THE
Daredevil
BOOK
FOR
Anglers

THE Daredevil BOOK FOR Anglers

Cunning Strategies That Fish Don't Know About

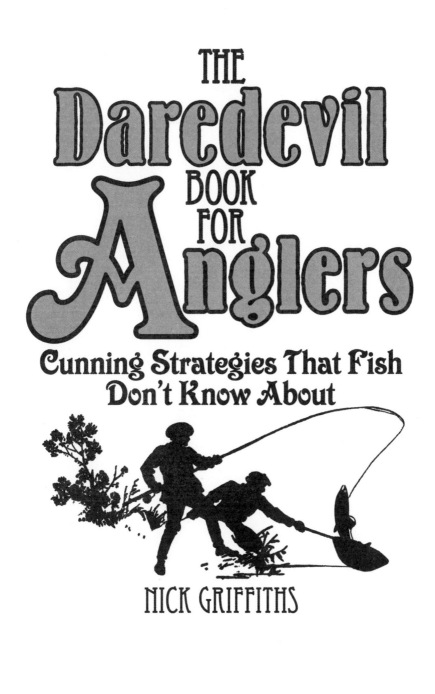

NICK GRIFFITHS

ARCTURUS

Nick Griffiths is an author and journalist because NASA wouldn't let him be an astronaut. He has written *The Daredevil Book for Cats*, *The Daredevil Book for Dogs*, *Dalek I Loved You: A Memoir* and *Who Goes There* (both based around Doctor Who), as well as the comic novel *In the Footsteps of Harrison Dextrose*, while writing largely for *Radio Times*. He owns a cat named Columbo, who has failed to solve any murder cases, and he has been banned from national and international fishing competitions for spiking his rivals' groundbait.

Illustrator **David Mostyn** began his career as a commercial artist in advertising, then moved into publishing and set up his own company Mostyn Partners in 1977. David has worked for 30 years in comic strips, producing drawings for DC Thomson, Marvel Comics and DC Comics, among others. He is married with two children and a cat, and lives in Oxford. This is his fourth Daredevil book.

ARCTURUS

This edition published in 2010 by Arcturus Publishing Limited
26/27 Bickels Yard, 151–153 Bermondsey Street,
London SE1 3HA

No fish were harmed in the making of this book

To find out more about sustainable fishing visit http://www.fishonline.org

Copyright © 2010 Arcturus Publishing Limited
Illustrations © 2010 David Mostyn

ISBN: 978-1-84837-546-8
AD001472EN

Printed in China

CONTENTS

INTRODUCTION

Hi, my name's Jim and I'm an angling addict. Show me a puddle and I'll drop a worm in it. Can't help myself. I'll fish anywhere that has water. (Except the loo.)

Why such addiction? It's that buzz of first feeling a fish take your bait, when the adrenalin kicks in and your head feels like it's been pulled off and dumped in a bowl of bees. On the rare occasions that I don't catch something, I will admit that white lies can creep in. Like the last time I drew a blank I went home via the fishmonger's, presented the wife, Sandra, with a ten-pound salmon – though I'd been coarse fishing she was none the wiser – and told her I'd landed it after an epic three-hour battle.

Not that I don't appreciate her support as she puts up with my repeated absences while feigning an interest. Whenever I've been fishing, I always make sure to bring her back a little gift. Most recently it was a swim-feeder. And before that a disgorger.

Angling, of course, is not the hippest of sports. It's not skateboarding, or free running. It's not even crochet. But I love it, and if you're reading this book I bet that you love it too. If I could shake your hand I would do, but I don't know where you are (or indeed where you've been). And I've just had my own mitts in a wormery, so it's probably for the best.

Still, the perceived image problems of our sport don't worry me. I'm comfortable with who I am. The wife says I look a bit like George Clooney in the right light, though I would never be so bold. (Admittedly she didn't say what the right light was.) It's out fishing when I really come alive: I'm a panther stalking its prey, with the patience of a polar bear, the eyesight of an eagle and the reflexes of a goat. Yes, a goat! If you think that goats don't have great reflexes, just you try climbing the higher slopes of a treacherous mountain and not falling off.

If you want proof, here's a recent photograph of myself.

Hmm, perhaps not the best example. It was a bit wet that day.

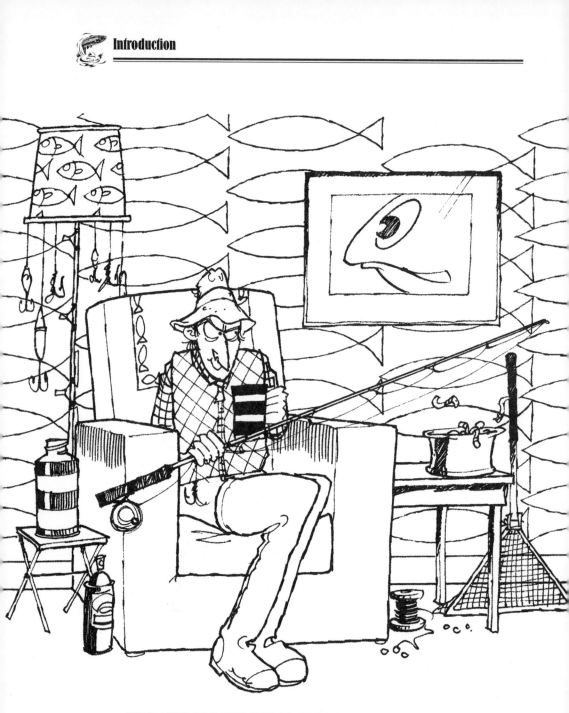

THE AUTHOR RELAXING ON A RARE DAY AT HOME
WHEN HE COULDN'T GO FISHING

Anyway, before I depart into the very depths of this great tome, let me first congratulate you on buying what many* agree to be the best manual on angling available to humanity.

(* 2009 SURVEY, 'IS THIS THE BEST MANUAL ON ANGLING AVAILABLE TO HUMANITY?'. RESPONDENTS (1), 'SANDRA', REPLIED 'YES', ALBEIT IN A SLIGHTLY ROBOTIC VOICE.)

Among these fine pages you will find my own hints and tips on catching the very biggest fish, whether you are game fishing, coarse fishing or out on the ocean waves. What else? I'll tell you:

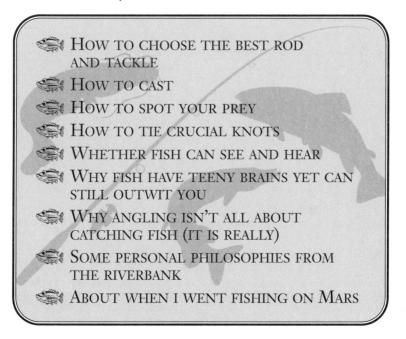

HOW TO CHOOSE THE BEST ROD AND TACKLE

HOW TO CAST

HOW TO SPOT YOUR PREY

HOW TO TIE CRUCIAL KNOTS

WHETHER FISH CAN SEE AND HEAR

WHY FISH HAVE TEENY BRAINS YET CAN STILL OUTWIT YOU

WHY ANGLING ISN'T ALL ABOUT CATCHING FISH (IT IS REALLY)

SOME PERSONAL PHILOSOPHIES FROM THE RIVERBANK

ABOUT WHEN I WENT FISHING ON MARS

Perhaps there's just enough space left here to tell you about the time I ended up hooking a 300lb conger eel, which I fought for two days, then gutted with a penknife and cooked al fresco in an old metal bath I found by the shoreside using driftwood as fuel... No, my editor's making a vigorous, throat-slashing gesture behind me, so I'll just have to save that for a later date.

Jim

THE ORIGINS OF FISHING

Darwin suggested that humans evolved from the things that crawled out of the primeval swamp, which were essentially fish that had grown funny little legs. So it follows that humans evolved from fish. QED.

But what's this funny-little-legged fish-thing going to eat? Why, fish, of course. (In the animal kingdom, eating one's relatives is not even frowned upon!) There's a problem, however.

How is that F-L-L F-T ever going to handle the intricacies of casting? It doesn't even have a rod! But all is not lost. Remember that classic diagram of the evolution of man? Here it is again, to remind you:

Our friend above is only halfway along that evolutionary scale. Move the clock forward a few hundred years – to somewhere around 1962, I'd reckon – and he's a fully-fledged human being with proper arms and legs, and the capability of buying a rod and tackle from his local angling emporium. Now he's in! From once being a fish, he is now fishing.

And those, my friends, are the origins of fishing. QED (ish).

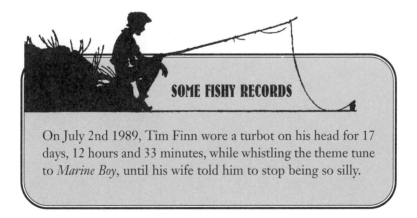

SOME FISHY RECORDS

On July 2nd 1989, Tim Finn wore a turbot on his head for 17 days, 12 hours and 33 minutes, while whistling the theme tune to *Marine Boy*, until his wife told him to stop being so silly.

HOW I BECAME HOOKED

here did my love of fishing come from? Well, it didn't just come from nowhere, did it? I imagine we all have a tale such as this...

Let me take you back to my childhood. Some big boys punched me and later I wet the bed... No, hang on, that's the wrong story.

It was a time of few friends and social naivety (and I'm fine with that because it's oh so different now). I'm ten years old and Dad's taking me on my first fishing trip, to a little lake in the countryside. My fishing gear comes plastic-packed, basic in the extreme: a two-piece rod, a reel for kids, a couple of floats, a small circular box of weights and half a dozen hooks. I gaze at it in wonder. It's like nothing I've ever seen.

How does it work? (No idea.) What does it do? (Collect radio signals from the cosmos?) How many fish will I catch? (What's a fish?) How huge will they be? (Bigger than me?) Will I even be able to lift them? (No. Yes. No. Maybe.) My head is full of dreams.

We find a space at the lakeside and break open the kit. I see other children, lines already in the water. The lake surface is calm, sunlight dancing among the few ripples, birdsong in my ears. I am at one with nature.

Which is great, because I want to catch nature and hit it on the head.

'Come on, Dad, hurry up!' I urge my father, as he squints through his spectacles to tie a knot, cursing under his breath. I pass the time by playing with some maggots in a green tub. Maggots are great, I decide. Until one falls down my vest and I run around in circles, waggling my arms like a small girl while screaming. Finally our tackle is ready. I pierce a maggot on to the hook and some goo comes out. *'Eugh!'* I go, hugely impressed. Now what?

Casting, as you know, requires the perfect balance of momentum and timing. It requires co-ordination and dexterity. It requires art, my friend.

I attempt to launch the bait as if I am launching a potato at Pluto. Consequently my float and bait sploosh loudly into the water not half a yard from my feet. Several further attempts produce the same result. Dad takes over. He's fished a few times in his past, though not recently enough to be any good at it.

Ten minutes later – though it feels like ten hours – Dad has broken my rod in two over his knee and has had to borrow a rod from the kid next door. Well, when I say 'borrow', it was more 'extort': Dad threatened to tell the lake owner he'd seen the kid wee in the water.

But he can't cast that rod, either, so Dad has an idea. *'If the fish won't come to us, we'll go to the fish!'* he announces. *'We'll hire a boat!'*

Which is when I discovered that my Dad can't row. We went around in

FISHY FACTS by DB Hartley

You might remember JR Hartley from such books as *Fly Fishing* by JR Hartley, *Look, I Caught One!* by JR Hartley, *Gah, My Fly Got Caught in a Tree* by JR Hartley, *Pesky Fly, Come Out!* by JR Hartley, and *Has Anyone Got a Ladder?* by JR Hartley.

To be fair, we're not related and, to be honest, I know a little less about angling than he did. However, we share a surname which is a qualification of sorts. So here is the first of my Fishy Facts:

❶ The carp is so-named because it grumbles a lot. Carping – see? Obviously you can't understand them because you don't speak Fish, but if you were another carp in a carp pond, all you'd hear would be, 'Call this a pond? I've seen bigger puddles!' and 'Where's my tea, love?'

circles for ages and he swore so much that I had to put my fingers in my ears. Then he knocked a duck unconscious with an oar, which is when the man from the RSPCA (Royal Society for the Prevention of Cruelty to Animals) intervened.

While Dad and the man from the RSPCA are arguing, the father of the kid next door, whose rod Dad had borrowed/extorted, comes back. The kid tells him what happened, and suddenly this burly bloke is wading into the shallows, with every intention of knocking Dad's block off.

Burly Bloke and RSPCA Man drag us ashore, shouting, while my Dad tries to ward them off with an oar. I leap out and cower on the bank… and notice something moving. A small fish lies on the bank, flapping uselessly. It had been washed up by the bow wave from our boat as it was being beached.

'*Dad! Dad!*' I cry. '*We've caught one!*'

Everyone stops fighting and becomes an expert on fishing.

'*Oh, that's a tench,*' says Burly Bloke.
'*It's not, it's a perch,*' says RSPCA Man.
'*Nonsense, the perch's fins are more golden. That's a roach,*' says Dad.
'*I caught this bream once…*' goes Burly Bloke, and they're off, suddenly the best of buddies.

I ignore them and gaze in wonderment at this scaly, shiny, gorgeous creature. This big – well, quite big – tench/perch/roach. It was mine. I had caught it (sort of). And there and then I understood.

I was hooked.

CHOOSING A ROD

There are all sorts of rods, for all types of fishing, available in all shapes and sizes. Well, not so much shapes – they all tend to be long and pointy. Anyway. Here are just a few examples:

- Match rods
- Float rods
- Boat rods
- Trout rods
- Salmon rods
- Carbon rods
- Fibreglass rods
- Hot rods
- Bamboo sticks

I could go on…

But I won't. These have all been developed for certain types of angling. However if you're prepared to hunt around, you can find still more specialized rods. For instance, there are rods for:

- Catching female tench with a wandering eye and a penchant for sweetcorn
- Catching a conger eel whose lip has been cut in a fight
- Catching dace with an inferiority complex
- Catching sturgeon who haven't noticed the 't' in their name and think they'd be great in an operating theatre
- Catching golden trout who were christened – but have since rejected the name – Nigel

See what I mean?

But my personal recommendation is this one – an all-purpose rod that should suit all levels and pretty much guarantees a fish, whether they're biting or not:

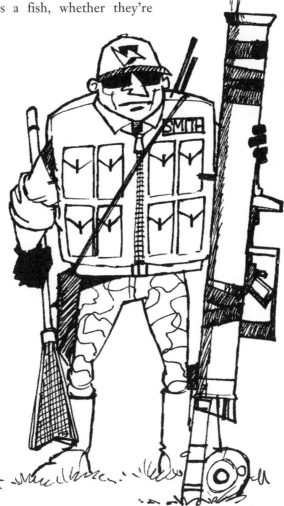

Note: To use this rod you will need a firearms licence as well as a fishing licence. Don't get nabbed by the bailiffs! (Or indeed the FBI.)

FISHY FISH: INTRODUCTION

Did I mention that I can talk to the fishes? [ER. IS THIS ANOTHER OF YOUR LITTLE ANGLING 'WHITE LIES'? – ED.] If you don't believe me, try asking my goldfish, Beryl.

Ah, sorry. Of course you can't. Allow me…

> ME: **Beryl, can I talk to the fishes?**
> BERYL: *Yes.*
> ME: **See?**

HE CAN TALK TO THE FISHES YOU KNOW!

How did this come about, you might be wondering. [IT HAD CROSSED MY MIND – ED.] It happened a few years back, when I landed a big carp in a lake at Newport Pagnell. Took a while to heave him in, and when he lay there on the bank, breathing heavily, I said out loud – talking to myself, really – **'Nice fight'**. And the big fish goes, *'Thank you.'*

Well, I couldn't believe it!

> **'Did you just say that?'** I asked the carp.
> *'Who else did you think it was?'* the carp replied.
> **DUMBFOUNDED!**
> **'I can talk to the fishes!'** I spluttered.
> *'I think it's more that I can talk to the humans,'* averred the big fish. And we argued for a while.
> Anyway, I wanted to take that carp home, put him in a tank and show off my gift to the world. That fish would have made me rich. But he said to me, *'You have to put me back, I'm gasping here. If you put me back I promise I'll come to the bank and talk to you, anytime you call.'*
> I couldn't bring myself to harm that amazing fish, so I did as he asked. And as he was swimming away, he lifted his head out of the water one final time and went, *'SUCKER!'*

That was the last I saw of him. [HOW CONVENIENT – ED.] But it's OK, because I found I can talk to all the other fishes!

So I shall use my remarkable gift for your benefit. Authors of angling books often have pages of fish-based facts: where a species of fish is found, what size they can grow to, that sort of thing. All rather repetitive and boring. [WELL, AND QUITE USEFUL – ED.]

Instead of all that waffle, I shall interview fish for you!

It doesn't get much more insightful or original than that. Ever heard what a plaice has to say for itself? Or a mackerel? Or a flying fish? Well, now's your chance. And it won't get much more in depth than this...

[SORRY ABOUT THIS – ED.]

FISHY FISH

Plaice

NAME: **Plaice**
LATIN NAME: *Uglias sinnus*
ENVIRONMENT: **Sea**

PROFILE

MOST LIKELY FOUND: Moping around
TEMPERAMENT: Glum
FAVOURITE TV SHOW: *The Addams Family*
FAVOURITE BOOK: *101 Beauty Tips*
IDEAL BIRTHDAY PRESENT: Paper bag
LUCKY NUMBER: n/a
HUMAN HERO: John Merrick, the Elephant Man
MOST LIKELY TO SAY: 'Do my eyes look big in this?'
LEAST LIKELY TO SAY: 'Mirror, mirror, on the wall…'
BEST SERVED WITH: Wilted spinach, black butter,
slice of lemon

MY INTERVIEW

ME: **So, plaice…**
PLAICE: *Do you think I'm ugly?*
ME: **Er…**
PLAICE: *You do!*
ME: **I didn't say that.**
PLAICE: *I could see it in your eyes!*
ME: **I wouldn't mention eyes if I were you.**

PLAICE: *What's wrong with my eyes?*
ME: **Have you heard of comedian Marty Feldman?**
PLAICE: *Who?*
ME: **Don't worry about it.**
PLAICE: *What's wrong with my eyes?*
ME: **Well. They are a touch boggly.**
PLAICE: *They're not!*
ME: **Do you know what boggly means?**
PLAICE: [Pause] *No.*
ME: **It means sticky-outy in funny directions.**
PLAICE: *You think I'm bad. Have you seen the turbot?*
ME: **I have.**
PLAICE: *And?*
ME: **Well, I think you're tastier.**
PLAICE: *You eat me?!*
ME: [Coughs]

TYPES OF ANGLER

People come in all shapes and sizes, some of them are nice and some of them are complete gits. So it is with anglers.

❶ The Over-equipped Amateur

To make up for being useless at fishing, has bought every possible angling gadget. However, fails to know how any of them work, and is likely to be found fishing with the keep net while someone else is using the rod as an aerial for their portable telly. Other anglers eye him with a mixture of envy, frustration and wanton animosity.

❷ The Family Man

Sees angling as a day out for the family rather than an artful sport that requires peace, concentration and no children to be playing Dunk Your Sister next to the float. Never catches anything and conclusively ensures that no one else catches anything either.

➌ The Smug Git

Actually rather good at fishing and makes sure that everyone else knows it. Is the first to ask the question, 'Caught anything yet?', safe in the knowledge that he has caught plenty. Spends much of the time pointedly pushing around a supermarket trolley full of fish, and making much of the fact that the effort is making his arms ache.

4 The Expert Caster

Could hit a small coin with a maggot at 100 paces, or cast a fly into the wind which dances as if it were performing ballet in front of some royals. Always stands where everyone else can see him. Makes others feel as if they are casting boulders using roof beams while dressed as the front half of a pantomime elephant. A noticeable hindrance to the angling self-esteem.

⑤ The Over-excitable Novice

Anglers generally reel in a fish with a modicum of decorum, endeavouring to keep their adrenalin-fuelled excitement in check. Not this chap. A loud shriek accompanies his bite, followed by delirious shouts of 'I've got one! I've got one!' and much jumping up and down. In the unlikely event that the fish is landed amid all that commotion, tends to require open-heart surgery not long afterwards.

⑥ The 'Jim'

A hale and hearty angler, not one prone to boasting or anything like that, who has just enough tackle for the task in hand, as well as a well-stocked (by Sandra) lunch bag, his special comfy fishing chair, and (admittedly) a portable telly and satellite dish, so he can watch fishing programmes from around the world, as he fishes – which isn't overkill. No way would he ever video himself fishing, then watch that while fishing. No siree. This man has fishing taped.

CHOOSING A REEL

Your choice of reel is as crucial as your choice of rod, so it's vital to get it right. And as with rods, there are many types available.

PROFILE

- Parallel reel
- Mirror reel
- Tandem reel
- Closing reel
- Sausage reel

Personally, I'd go for this one, the Highland reel, which suits most challenges (particularly when you're trying to entertain your Scottish auntie). [NOW YOU'VE REALLY LOST IT – ED.]

CHOOSING FISHING TACKLE

I've loved fishing tackle shops ever since I was knee high to a grasshopper. (It was a pretty unusual grasshopper. Its parents disowned it and other grasshoppers would mutter 'Freak' under their breath as it hopped past.)

I think of them as emporia, which perfectly conjures up that image of a treasure trove of delights. So much... stuff! All the colours and the varnish, lures here, artificial flies there, weights and rods everywhere. So many little drawers and compartments to be investigated, so many glass lids to be lifted. Walls covered from floor to ceiling with gadgets and devices.

What do they all do, even? Who cares! Here's my motto:

BUY FIRST,
ASK LATER

It's the angler's dreamland. I own so much fishing tackle I have to store it in a series of hangars vacated by NASA's rocket builders. You should start smaller – but what do you need? Here's a handy checklist, which has the ring of poetry for me:

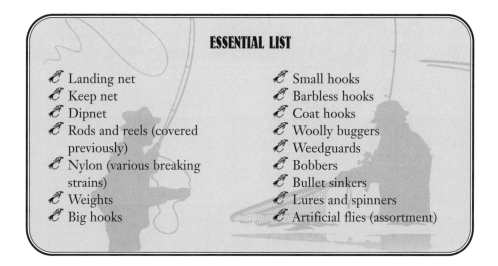

ESSENTIAL LIST

- Landing net
- Keep net
- Dipnet
- Rods and reels (covered previously)
- Nylon (various breaking strains)
- Weights
- Big hooks
- Small hooks
- Barbless hooks
- Coat hooks
- Woolly buggers
- Weedguards
- Bobbers
- Bullet sinkers
- Lures and spinners
- Artificial flies (assortment)

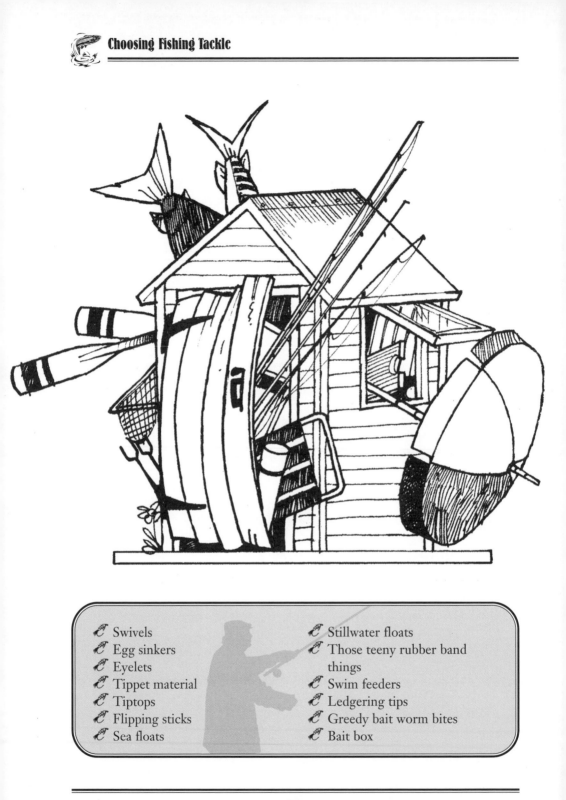

- 🐟 Swivels
- 🐟 Egg sinkers
- 🐟 Eyelets
- 🐟 Tippet material
- 🐟 Tiptops
- 🐟 Flipping sticks
- 🐟 Sea floats
- 🐟 Stillwater floats
- 🐟 Those teeny rubber band things
- 🐟 Swim feeders
- 🐟 Ledgering tips
- 🐟 Greedy bait worm bites
- 🐟 Bait box

- Live bait (worms, maggots, maddies, baby rags)
- Dipbait
- Flutterbait
- Jerkbait
- Stinkbait
- Angleworms
- Night-crawlers
- Zug bugs
- Bass assassins
- Peacock ladies
- Priests
- Bell sinker
- Catapult
- Rod rest
- Bite alarms
- Personal alarm
- Sense of alarm
- Alarming tendency to fall asleep
- Bite to eat
- Mosquito repellent
- Fly spray
- Reddy-pak chair
- Vacuum flask
- Outboard motor (in bits)
- Oars
- Otolith
- Rowlocks
- Epoxy resin
- PFDs and lifejackets
- Buoyancy bags

- Plastic bags
- Bags of old rubbish
- Varnish
- Vanish
- Sunglasses
- Sunscreen
- Sonar
- Plumb line
- Depth charges
- Crystal wagglers
- Backlash
- Spaghetti
- Professional overrun
- Puzzled expression
- Number of containers
- Number for Ikea customer services
- A Swedish person
- Swedish-English dictionary
- Different puzzled expression
- Armchair (to slump into)
- Head (to scratch)
- A bin
- A binbag
- Another bin
- More binbags
- Livebox
- Deadbox
- Any number of old boxes (sizes various)
- Everything else in the shop

SORRY, I JUST COULDN'T HOLD BACK IN THE END.

TYPES OF ANGLING

No. 1

Coarse Fishing

Where's it practised?
In freshwater lakes and rivers.
What can I catch?
Anything but trout and salmon (see Game Fishing). So stuff like carp, tench, dace, perch, etc.
How?
Float fishing, spinning or ledgering.
Why?
It's a fair point, since coarse fish are generally returned to the water and watching a float for ages can be blummin' boring.
Who was the first president of the United States?
George Washington.
What's the capital of Ecuador?
Is it Quito?
You tell me.
Hang on, these are supposed to be questions pertinent to coarse fishing!
Tee hee.

THE TYPICAL COARSE ANGLER LOOKS A BIT LIKE THIS.

He doesn't appear to be doing much fishing.
Looks can be deceptive.
They can.
But not in this case, I'd suggest. Coarse anglers use alarms to tell them when they have a bite. Saves watching a float or swing-tip for ages.
And allows them to drink loads of beer, then take a nap?
Not all coarse anglers look like that. That one appears to be a bit of an alcoholic.
Why not just set an alarm for when the fishmonger opens

and cut out all the rod-based shenanigans?
Because you don't generally eat coarse fish!
Then what's the point?!
You just don't get it, do you?
No!
Are you my wife in disguise?
No!
Then I suggest you read my chapter entitled 'Fishing – It's Not All About Catching Fish' (see page 148).
I will do!
Good.
Good!
Yes it is.
Can we move on to the next topic now?
Please do.

SIZE IS EVERYTHING

J ust as a fish someone else catches can never be too small, so the fish you're after can never be quite big enough.

The One That Got Away is easily demonstrated by holding out your arms to their fullest extent and embroidering your fishy tale like the Bayeux tapestry – no one will believe you anyway so you might as well go for broke.

But when you do finally land your fine finned friend, it's time to take his picture – the world must never be allowed to forget your dazzling minute of triumph. The fishing photograph is the most important part of any fishing expedition and its importance cannot be overstated.

But what happens if your fish is on the puny and undernourished side, a blot on your honour and a living mockery of your claims to be a top fisherman?

Fear not. Follow the instructions below and a stickleback will instantly come to resemble a prize pike, and that sickly, emaciated tench will transform into a close relative of the great white, or so it will seem.

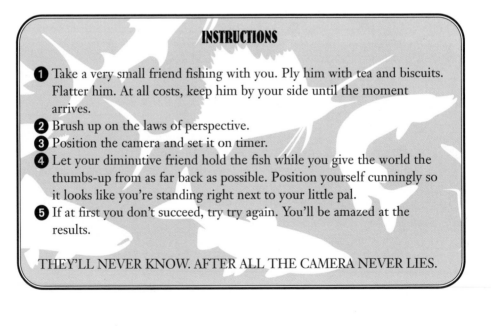

INSTRUCTIONS

1. Take a very small friend fishing with you. Ply him with tea and biscuits. Flatter him. At all costs, keep him by your side until the moment arrives.
2. Brush up on the laws of perspective.
3. Position the camera and set it on timer.
4. Let your diminutive friend hold the fish while you give the world the thumbs-up from as far back as possible. Position yourself cunningly so it looks like you're standing right next to your little pal.
5. If at first you don't succeed, try try again. You'll be amazed at the results.

THEY'LL NEVER KNOW. AFTER ALL THE CAMERA NEVER LIES.

WHAT TO WEAR

It's crucial to kit yourself out with the correct fishing outfit. Not just because you need to have all the right bits of equipment on you, and readily to hand, but because if you don't you'll look like an amateur.

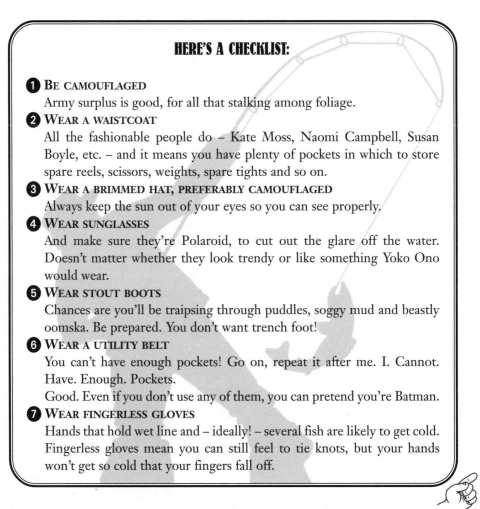

HERE'S A CHECKLIST:

1 BE CAMOUFLAGED
Army surplus is good, for all that stalking among foliage.

2 WEAR A WAISTCOAT
All the fashionable people do – Kate Moss, Naomi Campbell, Susan Boyle, etc. – and it means you have plenty of pockets in which to store spare reels, scissors, weights, spare tights and so on.

3 WEAR A BRIMMED HAT, PREFERABLY CAMOUFLAGED
Always keep the sun out of your eyes so you can see properly.

4 WEAR SUNGLASSES
And make sure they're Polaroid, to cut out the glare off the water. Doesn't matter whether they look trendy or like something Yoko Ono would wear.

5 WEAR STOUT BOOTS
Chances are you'll be traipsing through puddles, soggy mud and beastly oomska. Be prepared. You don't want trench foot!

6 WEAR A UTILITY BELT
You can't have enough pockets! Go on, repeat it after me. I. Cannot. Have. Enough. Pockets.
Good. Even if you don't use any of them, you can pretend you're Batman.

7 WEAR FINGERLESS GLOVES
Hands that hold wet line and – ideally! – several fish are likely to get cold. Fingerless gloves mean you can still feel to tie knots, but your hands won't get so cold that your fingers fall off.

NOW, PUT ALL THAT TOGETHER AND WHAT HAVE YOU GOT?

Now, can anyone explain to me why I have been stopped by the police on more than a dozen occasions? I recall one time…

POLICE OFFICER: **Excuse me, sir. Could you tell me where you're going?**
ME: *I'm going fishing, officer.*
POLICE OFFICER: **Then would you mind explaining to me why you're dressed like Johnny Rambo?**
ME: *Am I?*
POLICE OFFICER: **Sir, are you affiliated to any radical paramilitary group?**

ME: *No!*
POLICE OFFICER: **Do you have any weapons in your vehicle?**
ME: *No!*
POLICE OFFICER: **Bazooka, rocket launcher, mortar…?**
ME: *NO!*
POLICE OFFICER: **High explosives?**
ME: *NO!*
POLICE OFFICER:Anthrax, sarin…?
ME: *All I have is my fishing tackle!*
POLICE OFFICER: **A likely story.**
ME: *I'm going fishing!*
POLICE OFFICER: **Did you vote for any extreme right-wing organization at the last election, sir?**
ME: *I'm sorry?*
POLICE OFFICER: **Step out of the car, please, sir.**
ME: *Look, what's this all abou…*
POLICE OFFICER: **STEP OUT OF THE CAR!**
[I STEP OUT OF THE CAR]
POLICE OFFICER: **JESUS!** [POLICE OFFICER DRAWS GUN]
POLICE OFFICER: **DOWN ON THE GROUND! NOW! HANDS BEHIND YOUR BACK!**
ME: [MUFFLED] *This is my fishing outfit!*

HOW TO FIND FISH IN THE SEA*

(* SOUNDS TRICKY, DOESN'T IT?**)

(** IT IS.)

(SO, HOW IS IT DONE?***)

(*** NO IDEA!)

I'm joking, of course. I have every idea. Sea fishermen use a very long pair of binoculars, which they dunk beneath the water surface, to see far, far down into the depths. A bit like this:

I'M KIDDING, THAT'D BE STUPID (UNLIKE EVERYTHING ELSE IN THIS BOOK)

No, fishing boats are often equipped these days with a Fish Finder device, which shows a representation of the undersea on its screen. On that, the fisherman can see the sea depth as well as little graphic representations of shoals of fish, which the Fish Finder has picked up. So how does that work – how does the Fish Finder know where the fish are?*

(* IT'S A GOOD QUESTION.)

It's simple. An army of divers with clipboards and questionnaires patrols the undersea, taking surveys of the fish, their habitats, their size, etc.

And here's how it works. A diver/researcher will stop a shoal of fish and ask the following questions:

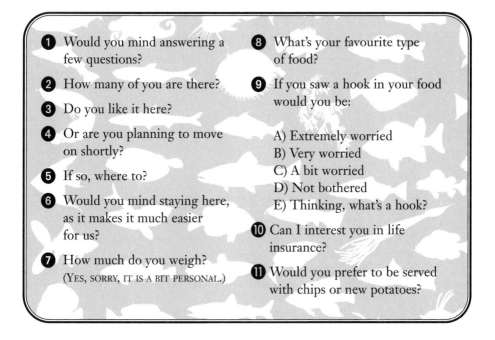

1 Would you mind answering a few questions?

2 How many of you are there?

3 Do you like it here?

4 Or are you planning to move on shortly?

5 If so, where to?

6 Would you mind staying here, as it makes it much easier for us?

7 How much do you weigh?
(YES, SORRY, IT IS A BIT PERSONAL.)

8 What's your favourite type of food?

9 If you saw a hook in your food would you be:

A) Extremely worried
B) Very worried
C) A bit worried
D) Not bothered
E) Thinking, what's a hook?

10 Can I interest you in life insurance?

11 Would you prefer to be served with chips or new potatoes?

The ocean's fish population is thus tracked and mapped out, and the information plotted on a fisherman's Fish Finder. Bumper catches all round!

Sea Fishing

Where's it practised?
In the sea. Duh.
What can I catch?
*The possibilities are practically endless, depending on where
you are in the world and what sort of rig you are fishing.
Beginners tend to start by landing a sackful of mackerel.*
How?
*Off a beach, when the possibilities are reduced, or from a boat,
generally by lobbing out a weight and bait or a lure.*
Why?
The hope of a record and fish for the pot.
How's the wife?
Yes, she's fine thanks.
Recovered from her operation?
How do you know about that?
Does she still blame you?
I've told you before – only questions related to fishing!
Snigger.

THE TYPICAL SEA ANGLER LOOKS A BIT LIKE THIS:

Er, isn't that more of a trawlerman?
Not really.
You sure?
Well that's how I like to go out to sea.
What, with a parrot on your hat?
Don't you knock Mr Micawber.
I'm sorry, who's Mr Micawber?
My lucky sea-fishing parrot.
You have a 'lucky sea-fishing parrot'?
Yes.
You're weird.
I don't believe so.
I do! Why?
Everyone does it.
Who exactly is 'everyone'?
Long John Silver...
And...?
Erm.
So Long John Silver mainly?
Hmm.
Who was a pirate rather than a fisherman?
But very famous.
And indeed fictional.
He's not!
He is! You look it up.
I will.
Actually, Mr Micawber looks more like a seagull than a parrot.
He does not.
Can we move on to the next chapter now?
Please do.

FISHY FISH

Mackerel

NAME: **Mackerel**
LATIN NAME: *Commonas muckus*
ENVIRONMENT: **Sea**

PROFILE

Most likely found: In front of the telly
Temperament: Hungry
Favourite TV show: Any
Favourite book: *Supersize Me*
Ideal birthday present: Some litter
Lucky number: 1,000,000
Human hero: Simon Cowell
Most likely to say: 'Pass the chips'
Least likely to say: 'Cowell's sartorial elegance is an inspiration to us all'
Best served with: Ginger, chilli and lime drizzle

MY INTERVIEW

ME: **Hi.**

MACKEREL: *Pass the remote control, will you?* [To 23 other mackerel] *Hoi – get out of the way of the telly!*

ME: **It's a bit crowded down here.**

MACKEREL: *Tell me about it. Hold on...* [Lunges at something, wolfs it down]

ME: **What happened there?**

MACKEREL: *Spotted a tasty bit of litter floating past. Here, do you want that fingernail?*

ME: **Well, yes. It is attached to my finger.**

MACKEREL: *Just asking.*

ME: **I don't see...**

MACKEREL: *Let me know next time you cut your nails, yeah?*

ME: **So you can eat the clippings?**

MACKEREL: *Waste not, want not.*

ME: **So you'll eat absolutely anyth...**

MACKEREL: [To 19 other mackerel] *Hoi, get out of the way of the telly!*

TYPES OF ANGLING

No. 3

Game Fishing

Where's it practised?
In freshwater lakes and rivers.
What can I catch?
Trout and salmon, viz. 'game' fish.
How?
By casting an artificial fly; spinners are looked down upon.
Why?
Because fly anglers can be a bit posh.
Are you a bit posh?
No!
That's not what Norman says.
Norman's lying!
Is he?
What has Norman been saying to you?
I thought all the questions had to be fishing-related?
That is!
My lips are sealed.
Why you...
Hehe.

THE TYPICAL GAME ANGLER LOOKS A BIT LIKE THIS:

Isn't that Prince Charles?
Yes, he fly-fishes.
So you're suggesting that the average game angler... is Prince Charles?
A bit.
So no one less regal is allowed to go fishing for trout and salmon?

Well, some people are.
Such as?
Queen Noor of Jordan.
I happen to know that Roger Daltry of The Who loves fly fishing, and he's not royalty.
Ah, but he's rock royalty.
Well, I didn't vote for him.
You don't vote for rock royalty!
All right, what about Brian May from Queen?
Queen's royalty. I imagine the fly would get caught in his hair when he cast.

I'm not talking about hair-based practicalities!
Right.
OK, what about President Barack Obama – would he be allowed to go game fishing?

I'd have to ask.
You'd have to ask?!
Has he got a crown?
This is ridiculous.
Shall we move on?
I think that's best.

MY AUSTRALIAN FISHING TRIP, 1995

They say there are 100 million species of animal that can kill or maim you in Australia. In fact the only non-toxic critter in the entire continent is the koala bear – which has been known to cuddle unsuspecting tourists to death! So it's a place where I was determined to wear a stout, knee-high pair of boots and bulletproof vest when I was lucky enough to visit back in '95.

As I was soon to discover, those dangerous critters included the fish. Here's one I landed within minutes of dropping a fly daintily on top of the water in New South Wales.

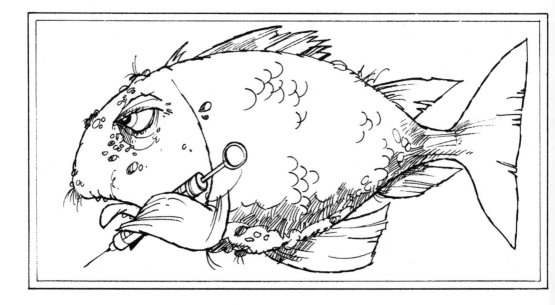

They call it the doctor fish, and it's been known to inject people around the mouth area, causing excruciating halitosis.

There was another one, which I narrowly avoided stepping on. Its real name is actually the creek halibut, but the locals call it the 'ankle snapper' for reasons I am about to explain.

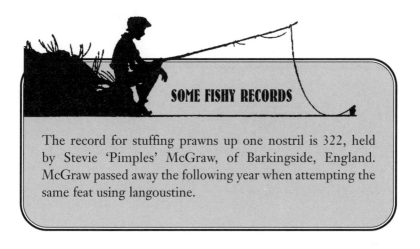

SOME FISHY RECORDS

The record for stuffing prawns up one nostril is 322, held by Stevie 'Pimples' McGraw, of Barkingside, England. McGraw passed away the following year when attempting the same feat using langoustine.

Every so often it hauls itself out of the water and sits on the bank waiting for some unsuspecting angler to step on it, then – wham! And back it slides into the water, to eat your foot over the course of a few days.

SO KEEP THOSE EYES PEELED.

But the trip wasn't all about fishing. It's important to grab some rest and relaxation, and I did visit the odd bar on my travels. One time, I was chatting with a lady by the name of Sheila – rest assured, I would never be unfaithful to the wife – and she was enthralled by my one-way conversation about the dietary habits of the tench, until she said she had to excuse herself. Shortly afterwards there was a commotion and I heard a shout: 'Some woman's just smashed her way out of the loo window!' Sheila must have bumped into a friend because I never did see her again.

Next day my plan was to go spearfishing. Then I started talking to an old Aussie sea salt, who gave me the lowdown on local species: box jellyfish, the blue-ringed octopus, stingrays, stonefish, toadfish, pufferfish, cobblers, carpet sharks, the Queensland groper, barracudas, weever fish, numbfish, great whites and even the venomous 'happy moments' fish, in other words nothing I couldn't handle. I wasn't afraid at all. However, I suddenly remembered the toxic effect all this fishing could be having on my marriage and hopped on the next available flight to England, stopping only to buy Sandra something nice in Duty-Free. And I vowed never again to visit Australia.

TYPES OF ANGLING

No. 4   Big Game Fishing

Where's it practised?
Far out at sea.
What can I catch?
Vast shark, tuna, barracuda, wahoo...
Isn't that last one an internet search engine?
No, that's Yahoo.
My mistake. It is.
Not on purpose, I trust.
I assume you've been big game fishing?
Is the Pope Catholic?
I've no idea. Is he Church of England?
All right. Do bears poop in the woods?
Would there be the option of an outside toilet?
I knew it – you're being facetious.
I wouldn't dream of it.
Do you know how annoying you are?
You hum it, I'll sing it.
This interview is terminated.
Fine by me.

THE TYPICAL BIG GAME ANGLER LOOKS A BIT LIKE THIS.

So you've done some big game fishing then?
Hello? I told you, the interview's terminated.
What's the biggest you've caught?
Come on, you know you want to...
It's eating away at you...
Bet there's a record in there somewhere...
Oh all right, damn you. Yes, I did catch a world-record marlin off the coast of Hawaii, when I went out fishing with Dog the Bounty Hunter, and Dog reckoned he was great at catching

fish cos he's so great at catching bad people and I said to him, 'That doesn't necessarily follow,' and we both had an 80-pound line and he got the first bite and he reeled in this blue marlin while the jangly tassles in his hair became sweaty and his blue marlin weighed 923 pounds and I scoffed at that and said I bet I can land a bigger one and lo and behold I felt this tug on my line like I'd hooked an undersea giant and I huffed and I puffed and... Are you still listening?

Oh, I'm sorry, I was just making a cup of tea. I thought you said the interview was terminated?

I'll get you for this.

TYPES OF ANGLING

No. 5   **Bigger-Than-That Game Fishing**

Where's it practised?
Really, really far out at sea.
What can I catch?
Veritable monsters. Denizens of the deep.
How?
*With squillion-pound breaking-strain line, a heart of steel
and bait the size of a whale shark.*
This is starting to sound a touch far-fetched.
It isn't!
It's another one of your 'stories', isn't it?
No!
All right, let's have a look at the typical bigger-than-that
game angler. OK.

THE TYPICAL BIGGER-THAN-THAT GAME ANGLER LOOKS A BIT LIKE THIS.

That's you, isn't it?
No.
It is!
Cough.

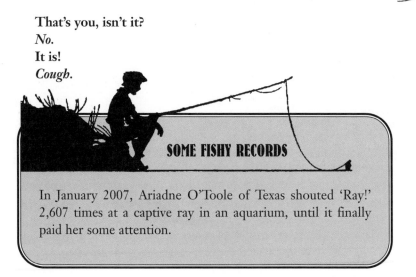

SOME FISHY RECORDS

In January 2007, Ariadne O'Toole of Texas shouted 'Ray!'
2,607 times at a captive ray in an aquarium, until it finally
paid her some attention.

HOW HOOKED ARE YOU?

nglers will always argue amongst themselves – or, more likely, bitch behind each other's backs – about who is the most dedicated or the most technically proficient, who has the most tackle, who caught the biggest fish, where the best fishing grounds are, blah blah blah. We're a competitive bunch.

But exactly how competitive are you?

I devised this handy multiple-choice quiz to sort the dabblers from the anglers, the spineless from the spined, the braggers from the bread-winners. Simply answer each question honestly, then tot up your score using the unique scoring system at the end. I warn you now: I scored 47 points, even though it's only out of 30.

QUESTION 1

What was the weight of the biggest fish you've ever caught?

A) 1,000 pounds
B) 100 pounds
C) 10 pounds
D) 'I'm afraid I lost it among the blades of grass.'

QUESTION 2

It's dusk and the fishery is closing – but you still haven't caught that monster you spotted lurking in the reeds. What do you do?

A) Pretend to pack up your kit, wish the bailiff a cheery goodnight and as he goes to shake your hand knock him unconscious with your priest. Tie him up and gag him, then carry on fishing

B) As above but without the knocking-unconscious bit – you just sneak back later

C) Abide by the rules of the fishery and gaily head home

D) Dusk?! You'd have been home by teatime, because your ickle tummy was wumbling

FISHY FACTS by DB Hartley

2 Why do eels go to all the trouble of swimming to the Sargasso Sea to spawn, when they could just spawn where they are? It's a funny story. On the beach at the Sargasso there used to be a HEEL BAR, where tourists could get their sandals and espadrilles mended. One day, in a storm, the 'H' blew off the sign, which then read EEL BAR. Well, the local eels couldn't believe their luck – at last they could drink a cooling beer as the sun warmed the sands! Eels from miles around came to sample the bar's delights, until they realized it still only mended shoes. But by then the rumour of eel booze had spread far and wide, and slow-witted eels still visit to this day.

3 Octopuses are highly susceptible to stress, perhaps because they are just too darned smart for their own good. A giant Pacific octopus built an exact replica of Milan opera house out of matchsticks at Fife Sea Life Centre, Scotland, while an enterprising mimic octopus with time on its hands has rewritten Beethoven's piano sonatas at a Louisiana theme park. So far no human being has been able to play any of them.

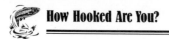

QUESTION 3

Where do you store your tackle?

A) You know the gigantic hangars where they build the Apollo rockets? When NASA stopped going to the moon, they sold those off. In there
B) In the garage
C) In a cupboard
D) 'Just my small fishing bag suffices.'

QUESTION 4

It's dawn and you've arrived at your local mega-lake. You're setting up your tackle when another angler arrives and begins doing the same, only more quickly. You know you want to get out on the lake first – so what's your plan?

A) Inquire innocently which boat he intends to use, then wee in its petrol tank when he's not looking
B) Get a blummin' move on so that you're in your boats at the same time. Treat the journey out into the lake like a powerboat race, barging and shaking your fist if required
C) Dash into a boat and head out on to the lake. You can finish setting up your tackle there, once you've bagged the best spot
D) Reason that it's a big enough lake for two people and shrug if your rival sets off first

QUESTION 5

An angler across the lake from you has landed a fish, while you haven't even had a nibble. Cheerily he lifts the fish out of the water to show you and gives you the thumbs-up. How do you react?

A) Storm over and start shouting, 'Oh, Mr Oneupmanship is it? Think you're better than me?! I'll show you!' Lob his fish back into the lake, break his rod over your knee and storm back to resume fishing
B) Flick him a finger or two back, then start fishing more determinedly than ever, scowling

C) Pretend you hadn't noticed

D) Hoist a thumb in reply and call across, 'Well done!'

QUESTION 6

Using your swish new Polaroids, you've spotted some large fish under the far bank. A fellow angler walks past and asks if you have any idea where the fish are. What do you do?

A) Kill him and hide his body in some bushes.

B) Tell him to mind his own business. 'Bloody cheek!'

C) Mention that you've seen a few over there, but he's just as likely to hook in elsewhere

D) 'There are some whoppers under the far bank. Here, why don't you have a few casts while I eat my sandwiches?'

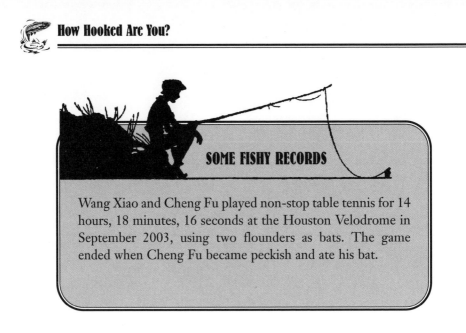

SOME FISHY RECORDS

Wang Xiao and Cheng Fu played non-stop table tennis for 14 hours, 18 minutes, 16 seconds at the Houston Velodrome in September 2003, using two flounders as bats. The game ended when Cheng Fu became peckish and ate his bat.

QUESTION 7

You're in a fishing competition. You're losing. What do you do?

A) Tell everyone within earshot that you've had a dodgy elbow for the past few days, which is affecting your cast. Then fall over clutching your left arm, crying weakly, 'Heart attack. Need ambulance'
B) Phone your partner and tell them to buy the biggest fish in the fishmonger's and bring them to you pronto. Pray they know the difference between seafish and freshwater fish
C) No need to panic, the competition's not over yet and there's a chance you might land something special
D) Quit and go home to do some knitting

QUESTION 8

How accurate is your casting?

A) 'I could land a maggot on a pinhead at 100 yards. Blindfolded'
B) 'If a fish rises, I'll hit the centre of those ripples'
C) 'If I'm within a few feet of where I intended, I'm pretty happy'
D) 'When I get this hook out of my eye I'll focus on your question'

QUESTION 9

Someone at the fishing club is spreading rumours that you've been exaggerating your catches...

A) Find out who the person is, dump the body of the angler from Q6 in their car boot and tip off the cops

B) Find out who the person is, swap their catch from some anchovies you found in your fridge, then tell the club captain that they've been exaggerating their catch

C) Keep schtum and vow never to exaggerate your catch again. At least you got away with it for a while

D) Hold your hands up, quit the club and depart in shame

QUESTION 10

Your partner's best friend is getting married but you'd rather go fishing. How do you play it?

A) Ring your partner's best friend and tell them that you've been having an affair with their fiancé/e for the past ten years and that you're deeply in love. Go fishing immediately afterwards

B) Tell your partner you've never liked their best friend, and if they make you go to the wedding you'll put your hand up after the bit where the vicar asks about anyone knowing why these two people shouldn't get married etc

C) Beg, plead, whine and huff before giving in

D) Go to the wedding. Well, it's the happiest day of someone's life!

SCORING SYSTEM: *If you answered:* A) Score 3 points B) Score 2 points C) Score 1 point D) Score 0 points. *Now calculate your total*
RATINGS GUIDE: 0–14 points – *Loser. Stick to the fishmonger's* 15–29 points – *Amateur. Where's your tenacity?* 30 points – *Hang on, are you me?! No, sorry, my mistake – I scored 47*

MY BRILLIANT IDEAS

No. 1

Super-Waders

I always look at waders and think, yes, they're deeper than Wellington boots, but are they really deep enough? What if I wanted to go fishing in a fjord? It strikes me that wader manufacturers haven't pushed the boat out far enough.

CALL THAT A PAIR OF WADERS?

THIS IS A PAIR OF WADERS!

FISHY FACTS by DB Hartley

4 Where did the phrase 'He sleeps with the fishes' come from? Well, some years ago there was an Italian gentleman by the name of Mario, who was so fond of his tropical fish that he would sleep in the fish tank. Then one night another Italian gentleman broke into Mario's house and shot him while he slumbered. The killer was stopped by the police who asked him to explain Mario lying lifeless in a fish tank, and he burbled out, 'He's sleeping with the fishes.' Amazingly, he got away with it because the cops failed to notice the bullet hole in Mario's forehead. Afterwards the phrase was adopted by a Mafia hitman trying to fob off the police.

5 In 1999, a family of turbot living under a pier in west Wales learnt how to play arcade games and became adept at turning a profit on the one-armed bandits. Using winnings they accumulated over a number of generations, they formed a syndicate to play the UK National Lottery and in 2004 they won a jackpot of £3.4 million which they invested in a private beach in Dubai. It's only because they refused publicity that no one has ever heard of these enterprising fish who now live as tax exiles.

It was using my own patented Super-Waders that I caught the legendary Loch Ness Monster, who had been hiding out at 20 fathoms since the dawn of time. I can tell you, it took a while to wade back to the bank and haul that critter out of the deep!

(If you wonder why you didn't read about that somewhere, I don't like to make a fuss so I popped him back. And there was no one around to take a photograph. Curse my luck!)

One tip before I go: don't wade out for miles then realize you need a wee – it's pretty claustrophobic in there.

FISHY FISH

Rainbow trout

NAME: **Rainbow trout**
LATIN NAME: *Vainus deludus*
ENVIRONMENT: **Freshwater**

PROFILE

MOST LIKELY FOUND: Pole-dancing
TEMPERAMENT: Delusional
FAVOURITE TV SHOW: *MacGyver*
FAVOURITE BOOK: *Cinderella*
IDEAL BIRTHDAY PRESENT: Galoshes
LUCKY NUMBER: 42
HUMAN HERO: Kermit
MOST LIKELY TO SAY: 'Do you like my scales?'
LEAST LIKELY TO SAY: 'Bag my face'
BEST SERVED WITH: Almonds

MY INTERVIEW

RAINBOW TROUT: *Who's more attractive, me or the brown trout?*
ME: **Well…**
RAINBOW TROUT: *Thought so!*
ME: **I hadn't decided yet!**
RAINBOW TROUT: *Do you like my shimmery skin?*
ME: **Very nice.**

RAINBOW TROUT: *See?*
ME: Yes, but the brown trout has those lovely golden tones and…
RAINBOW TROUT: *Oh, lovely golden tones, is it?*
ME: There's no need to get defensive.
RAINBOW TROUT: *I suppose you like the brown trout's red and black spots?*
ME: Well…
RAINBOW TROUT: *Would you like me to dance for you, is that it?*
ME: No!
RAINBOW TROUT: *You want me to pole-dance for you!*
ME: I certainly do not!
RAINBOW TROUT: *I know your type! Etc., etc.*

WHY I WOULD NEVER EXAGGERATE

It's not in my nature. Never would be, never will be. Some anglers... Oh all right then, all anglers – every damned one of them – are susceptible to it. All right, not susceptible... *driven* to it. They can't help themselves. It's like... It's like a *drug*. Need it, gotta have it. *Must exaggerate.*

BUT NOT ME. NOT NEVER.

What causes such wanton mendacity? Can't say I know. Maybe I'll never know. Oh all right... *I will never know. Cannot ever know.* Though the *need to know* claws at my insides, turns them inside out, spills my guts on a cold stone floor and runs fingers through them, seeking, searching, *craving* the truth, like some angling-based soothsayer.

And I cry out to the heavens:

> 'GIVE ME A SIGN! TELL ME WHY PEOPLE
> EMBELLISH QUITE MUNDANE STORIES TO MAKE
> THEM SOUND LIKE SOMETHING FROM A
> RUBBISH, OVERHEATED HOLLYWOOD MOVIE!
> TELL ME, DAMN YOU!'

But nothing. Nothing ever. It's like a void. Oh all right, it is a void. Blank, empty space, where a million souls wail for redemption and the night never ends. So cold. So very, very cold. So very, very, very cold. So very, very, very, very cold. So v... [YES, I THINK WE GET THE DRIFT – ED.]

How much colder can it get? None more colder, that's how much colder can it... Than it can... Can than colder... Anyway.

And in those very depths of despair I wonder. I wonder a lot. I wonder more than anyone else has ever wondered. Ever. I wonder why the angler stretches wide his arms to describe the length of his or her catch, when the outstretched rear pincers of the average passing earwig would just as easily do the job. *Why?*

And then I am in turmoil. In such exquisite pain. In purgatory. In hell. In the pits of hell. In the small hidden chamber beneath those pits that few are aware of. Then in the anteroom off that. And though I search for rooms further into the pits of hell I can find none. Not one. *I am as far into hell as one can possibly go.*

How I wish I could solve this mystery. Then I would become the world's greatest detective, like Sherlock Holmes, only I would wear a bigger hat. And my pipe would be nicer.

The Sign of Four? I'd solve *The Sign of Four Million.*

And I would declare to the world, with my arms open wide:

'YEAH, I CAUGHT A FISH AND IT WAS *THIS* BIG!
IT DAMNED WELL WAS!'

CARP FISHING TACTICS

The carp is among the wiliest of our scaly cousins, so I'm often asked, 'Jim, what tips can you give us on catching such an elusive yet rewarding fish?' I'll tell you.

1. Take time to look for the fish before setting up.

2. Catapult groundbait into your chosen swim. Little and often is best.

3. Fish several rods at different distances, then if one receives more attention you know how far from the bank the carp are feeding.

4. Carp love a bit of chilli in their diet, so mix in a little chilli powder with your bait to give it that extra kick.

5. Carp also love all things salty, so throw in some rock salt too.

6. Change your bait. Carp are the foodies of freshwater and quite like Jamie Oliver's recipes. Try something from Jamie's *Ministry of Food: Anyone Can Learn to Cook in 24 Hours* or *Jamie at Home: Cook Your Way to the Good Life*.

7. Ever considered that perhaps your wife might like some of that Jamie Oliver food, so why are you lobbing it pointlessly into a lake while the heavens open and a fat chap next to you tells you what happened in a recent episode of *Family Guy*, yet fails to make it sound funny?

8. Work out how many hours you have spent carp-fishing in the past ten years and wonder whether that was necessarily time well spent.

9. Change to a high-visibility bait.

10. Try a method feeder.

11. Change your rig system.

12. Allow your mind to slip back to 10 (above). Listen to the rain drip-drip-dripping on your hat.

13. Feel very alone.

14. Allow the chill to set into your bones.

15. Begin to shiver.

16. Come on, sort yourself out! You love carp fishing, you know you do! Try altering the distance between bait and hook bend.

17. Shiver some more as rain runs off your nose.

18. Stand up, throw your arms out and shout, 'Oh God NO! Why?'

19. Sit down, embarrassed by the stares of other anglers, yet somehow enlightened.

20. Start changing to a smaller hook, but halfway through tying the knot wonder: What's this all about? Why am I even here?

21. Look at your hands, which are red and shrivelled.

22. Abandon everything and walk to your car. Sit in the driving seat staring into space.

23. Turn the key in the ignition. Yeah, go on, start that engine! That's it! Course this is a great idea! Now drive that car over all your expensive carp-fishing tackle and onward into the lake! Do it! That'll show 'em! They'll never get away with it!

24. As your electrics short out and the engine seizes up, begin to wonder who exactly it was you were showing. Look sheepish.

25. Vow never again to think too hard about why it is you love carp fishing. Some things just are.

SOME ANGLING QUOTES

…and what they really mean.

'Somebody just back of you while you are fishing is as bad as someone looking over your shoulder while you write a letter to your girl' – ERNEST HEMINGWAY
Just because I like fishing, it doesn't mean I don't have a girlfriend

'It has always been my private conviction that any man who pits his intelligence against a fish and loses has it coming' – JOHN STEINBECK
You come home with no fish and I'll beat you up

'Fishing is the sport of drowning worms' – ANON
Hello, is that the police? Yes, I've caught nothing again and I'm being followed by John Steinbeck

'There are two types of fisherman: those who fish for sport and those who fish for fish' – ANON
If a sport fisherman invites you to a barbecue, expect burgers

'The charm of fishing is that it is the pursuit of what is elusive but attainable, a perpetual series of occasions for hope' – JOHN BUCHAN
Can you tell that I'm a writer?

"'I'm going out to fish," Simon Peter told them, and they said, "We'll go with you." So they went out and got into the boat, but that night they caught nothing' – JOHN 21:3
Simon Peter's boat was overcrowded; he wished he'd just said, 'No'

'An angler is a man who spends rainy days sitting around on the muddy banks of rivers doing nothing because his wife won't let him do it at home' – ANON
Wives don't mind having muddy riverbanks in the house, it's just their husbands' inactivity that galls them

'Fishing is a discipline in the equality of men – for all men are equal before fish' – HERBERT HOOVER
Those pesky fish don't seem to realize I'm the president!

'There's no taking trout with dry breeches' – MIGUEL DE CERVANTES
I'm so bad at fly fishing I have to wade in after the buggers

'Fishing is much more than fish. It is the great occasion when we may return to the fine simplicity of our forefathers'
– HERBERT HOOVER
My grandad was a bit of a thickie

'Nothing makes a fish bigger than almost being caught' – ANON
I've never heard of fish food

'Angling may be said to be so like the mathematics that it can never be fully learned'
– IZAAK WALTON
Don't talk to me about algebra

'If one really loves nature, one can find beauty everywhere'
– VINCENT VAN GOGH
I'll spout any old guff to take my mind off the dreadful stinging in my ear region

'One fish. Two fish. Red fish. Blue fish. Black fish. Blue fish. Old fish. New fish. This one has a little star. This one has a little car. Say! What a lot of fish there are' – DR SEUSS
I'm losing my mind

'A fishing pole is a stick with a hook at one end and a fool on the other' – SAMUEL JOHNSON
Just because I wrote a dictionary, I think I'm cleverer than everyone else

'The best way to a fisherman's heart is through his fly' – ANON
Er, yes, I think we'll leave this chapter there.

SHHHHH! (OR CAN FISH HEAR YOU?)

Ever noticed how anglers creep around on river banks and whisper to each other? As if the fish are listening in? But is all that subterfuge really necessary?

Can fish hear you?

Don't thank me, but I conducted some scientific experiments in this area, to find the answer for you.

EXPERIMENT 1:
Testing for the presence of ears

I picked up a live fish and looked for ears in its head region.
   I found none.
   This was my first big clue.

EXPERIMENT 2:
The blind whisper

Next, I put the same fish behind a screen, with a camera trained on it. Monitoring the fish's reaction on a computer, I sat the other side of the screen and began to whisper scurrilous rumours about its sex life. The fish did not react.

I then discovered that it was deceased (it having taken me so long to set up the camera, while said fish was out of water). So I tried the same experiment with a new fish.

Still it did not react.

This was my second big clue.

FISHY FACTS by DB Hartley

6 Why does something half-baked take the prefix cod, as in cod psychology? Because cod are pretty rubbish psychologists! I've heard cod trying to be all deep and the best they can do is, *'Life? Eh?'* and *'Well that's what happens, see?'* Never go to a cod if you have issues.

7 Whiting don't like halibut and no mistake. When a halibut intrudes on a whiting gathering, it is met by complete silence all round. No whiting will utter a sound until the halibut has moved on.

8 It once rained sardines in a small town in Texas. Local fisherman John Wayne Abattoir, who was prone to exaggeration, reported that it was raining tuna and a state of emergency was declared.

EXPERIMENT 3:
Shouting loudly

Finally I picked up the fish and shouted at it at close range:

'HELLO, MR FISH! CAN YOU HEAR ME, MR FISH? FISHY FISHY FISHY!'

The reaction? None. Not even a blink of an eyelid. [DO FISH HAVE EYELIDS? – ED.] This was my final big clue.

I can therefore scientifically, categorically state:

Fish cannot hear you.

(Still it looks swish and professional stalking along a river bank whispering, so go ahead and do it anyway. I know I do.)

SOME KNOTS

Mastering your knots is crucial to any angler. A knot that comes undone is a fish that gets away. That's why you should learn your knots and practise, practise, practise them. I locked myself in a Nissen hut with two pieces of string for seven weeks, and I didn't emerge until I knew every knot in the book and could tie them blindfolded, backwards, upside-down, sideways and while passing a friend their pencil case.

These are those knots. LEARN THEM!

BLOOD KNOT
For joining two lines together

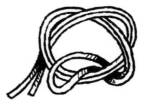

SURGEON'S END LOOP
Forms a loop at end of line

IMPROVED CLINCH
For tying hook to line

OH COME ON LOOP
When it all gets a bit fiddly

JUST GET IN THERE WILL YOU KNOT
When you start calling inanimate nylon *'stupid'*

SOD THIS I GIVE UP CLINCH
For throwing on the ground and storming out

FISHING AT NIGHT

Y ou can't beat a bit of fishing at night for atmosphere. The hoots of the owls, the wind through the trees, the petrifying cracks of twigs underfoot from unidentifiable sources, the nerve-shredding howls of perhaps wolves or bears... Actually, night fishing isn't for me.

But it may be for you, and if so there are a couple of potential hurdles to be aware of. So heed well these Before and After (as if seen through night-vision binoculars) shots of actual anglers...

1 Make sure you set up your gear and start fishing before night falls. You want to be certain you know where the watery bit is.

2 Also be sure you know what sort of fish you're likely to catch. You really don't want to be taken unawares in the darkness.

FISH IN CLASSIC LITERATURE

Moby Dick
BY HERMAN MELVILLE

Moby Dick is a whale (which isn't a fish, allegedly, but it sure looks like a big fish to everyone bar the finicky) who has bitten off Captain Ahab's leg. The Captain wants revenge so he sets sail in his boat to find Moby Dick. When he does so, the whale eats him. So much for revenge. But there is a twist in the tale.

In the whale's stomach, Ahab encounters the diminutive vegetarian, Moby, who gave the big whale its name (along with Dick of *The Dick van Dyke Show*). Moby introduces himself as a musician, but Ahab is suspicious because Moby is bald and he thought all musicians were hairy and wore beards.

So Moby, who had put on a bit of weight since retiring from showbiz, plays Ahab some soothing electronica which he had planned to flog to big companies for use in television adverts (before he was swallowed by Moby Dick) and Ahab is convinced. The two become firm friends.

However they discover there is a downside to being firm friends inside a whale when they are both dissolved by Moby Dick's stomach acid.

The Old Man and the Sea
BY ERNEST HEMINGWAY

A wise old fisherman named Santiago has gone for many days without catching anything and is in danger of starving to death. So he takes his boat out farther than ever before and hooks a giant marlin. For two days and nights the old man fights the big fish, and only on the third day, when he is on the point of exhaustion, does he manage to bring it alongside his boat. He is elated and wonders how much such a huge fish will fetch at market.

Then a boat run by some eco-warriors comes along and the eco-warriors point out to Santiago that the marlin is a non-sustainable species whose numbers have dwindled alarmingly due to overfishing. They harpoon the old man and set the marlin free.

SOME FISHY RECORDS

A grouper by the name of Sid stole into Buckingham Palace one night during June 2001, popped the crown on his head and passed himself off as the Duke of Edinburgh for 127 hours. He was only discovered because he didn't say anything untoward about visiting foreign dignitaries during all this time.

Pride & Parrotfish
BY JANE AUSTEN

Batty old Mrs Bennet is looking for suitors for her series of daughters. There is no shortage of willing volunteers, among them the wealthy square, Mr Bingley, who has a pathological fear of peanuts; Mr Wickham, who is a reincarnated goose; and Mr Darcy who is forever falling into water whilst wearing breeches. It is Mr Darcy who takes the eye of young Lizzie Bennet, and one day she falls into the water too, all accidental like. *'Oh, I didn't mean to fall in the water beside you, Mr Darcy!'* she tells Mr Darcy, even though that's a lie.

Just when Lizzie thinks she's got her man, Darcy feels something swimming around his breeches and sees that it is a parrotfish. *'My name is Mabel,'* says the parrotfish, batting false eyelashes. It is love at first sight and Mr Darcy and Mabel are married after a whirlwind romance. Mrs Bennet tries to console her daughter by telling her there are *'plenty more fish in the sea'*; however, the unfortunate turn of phrase leads Lizzie to kill herself.

Oliver Turbot
BY CHARLES DICKENS

Oliver Turbot says, *'Please sir, I want some more.'* Someone points out that he's a fish and shouldn't really be proffering bowls on dry land. Oliver goes hungry.

IN THE EVENT OF A SHARK ATTACK...

Speaking of dangerous animals, few come more dangerous than the deadly great white. If you don't believe me, watch *Jaws*, which has come to be recognized as a documentary by those in the know.

What should you do if you're out fishing and fall into shark-infested waters? Some people tell you to gouge an attacking shark's eyes, or to punch it on the nose. Complete rubbish!

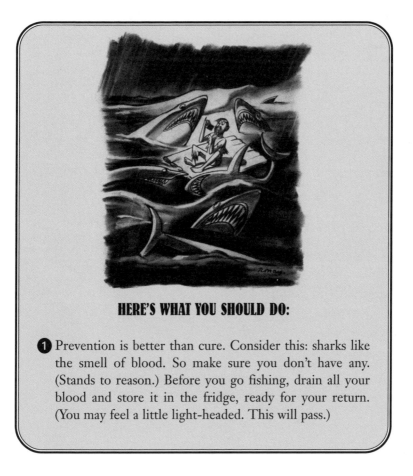

HERE'S WHAT YOU SHOULD DO:

❶ Prevention is better than cure. Consider this: sharks like the smell of blood. So make sure you don't have any. (Stands to reason.) Before you go fishing, drain all your blood and store it in the fridge, ready for your return. (You may feel a little light-headed. This will pass.)

❷ Always go shark fishing with a friend. If you feel yourself losing your balance on board, pull your friend into the water with you. Immediately your chances of being attacked are halved. (Should you both survive, be prepared for relations to be a bit strained.)

❸ OK, let's imagine you have foolishly failed to take either of the above preventative steps and are now in the water, being circled by a hungry shark. Think back to some of those magazine interviews with comedians you have read. How many recalled that their humour originated in the school playground, when they told jokes to stop bullies from picking on them? Lots – precisely!

And what is that circling shark but a big bully? So try telling it a shark-based joke. Example:

> *Where did the animals take refuge, two by two?*
> **In Noah's sh-Ark!**

4 Let's assume the shark didn't find that remotely funny. You may even have infuriated it. If so, whip out your underwater camera and take a digital photograph of the shark as it bears down on you, teeth bared. Now – quickly, before it bites your arm off – show it the photograph on the camera screen. Chances are the shark will feel pangs of guilt. How ugly it looks, all bloodthirsty like that. Violence never solved anything, the shark may realize. It may begin to wonder where all that pent-up rage came from. Was it mistreated by its father? Perhaps denied a sense of self-worth? Are there underlying issues here?

5 Alternatively it may have eaten your camera. Now you have problems. The vicious beast is so close you can see its teeth could do with a vigorous brushing. Chances are, that shark has never even flossed. So...

6 Try recommending a good dental hygienist. One good turn deserves another – the shark may leave you alone.

7 Still coming for you, eh? OK. Er. Have you tried punching it on the nose?

8 GOUGE ITS EYES! FOR GOD'S SAKE, GOUGE ITS EYES BEFORE IT'S TOO LATE!

9 Hello? ... Hello?

10 [GAZES AT SKY, WHISTLES.]

IF A FISH'S BRAIN IS THAT BIG AND MY BRAIN IS THIS BIG, HOW COME THEY KEEP OUTWITTING ME?

H aha, yes it's a puzzler, isn't it! Luckily I've worked it out. Let's look at a cross-section of a human brain and that of a halibut, side by side and roughly to scale...

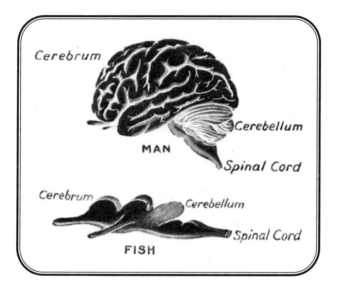

See what happens when we focus on the areas devoted to catching fish and to being caught? Though the halibut's brain is teeny compared to ours, all of its brain is devoted to cunning. Since humans have a few more things to do than that – walking to the shops, grumbling about chickens, to name but a couple – we can only devote a comparatively tiny portion to the art of angling. And that's why.

Of course, my brain looks more like this:

AMOUNT OF MY BRAIN
DEVOTED TO CATCHING FISH

See, half my brain focuses on catching fish – and that's why I'm so good at it.

[SINCE SO MUCH OF YOUR BRAIN IS DEVOTED TO FISHING, DOESN'T THAT MEAN YOU LACK BRAIN-POWER IN OTHER AREAS? – ED.]
Erm. See, half my brain focuses on catching fish – and that's why I'm so good at it.

[LET ME REPEAT THE QUESTION: SINCE SO MUCH OF YOUR BRAIN IS DEVOTED TO FISHING, DOESN'T THAT MEAN YOU LACK BRAIN-POWER IN OTHER AREAS? – ED.]
I don't follow.

[I DOUBTED THAT YOU WOULD. LET ME ASK YOU A QUESTION. WHAT IS 15 x 6? – ED.]
Eleventy seven? Threety none?

[AS I SUSPECTED. WHAT'S THE NAME OF THE PRIME MINISTER OF GREAT BRITAIN? – ED.]
Wilbur?

[IF I HAVE THREE BISCUITS AND YOU HAVE ONE, WHO HAS THE MOST BISCUITS? – ED.]
Has Wilbur been stealing my biscuits?

[I THINK WE'LL LEAVE IT THERE – ED.]

HOW TO SHOOT FISH IN A BARREL

FISHY FISH

Anglerfish

NAME: **Anglerfish**
LATIN NAME: *Whatthe &£$%us?*
ENVIRONMENT: **Dark bits of sea**

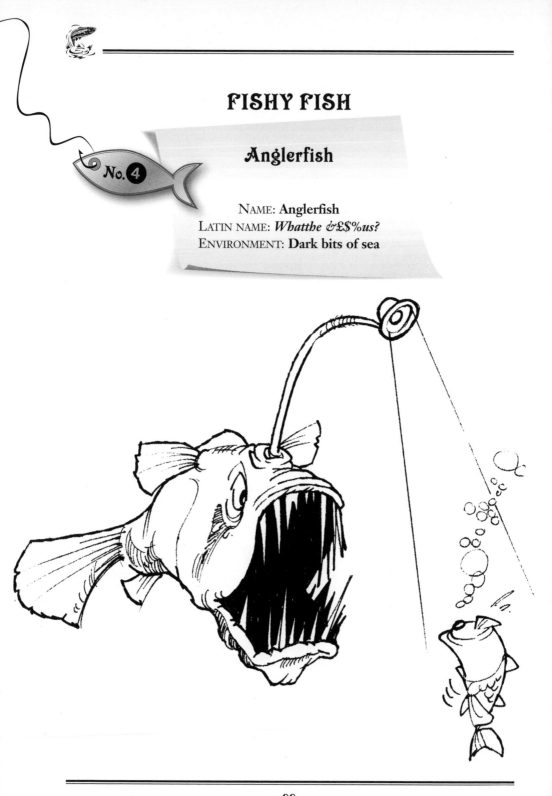

PROFILE

MOST LIKELY FOUND: Wandering down dark alleys at night
TEMPERAMENT: Ugly
FAVOURITE TV SHOW: *Total Fishing*
FAVOURITE BOOK: *Frankenstein*
IDEAL BIRTHDAY PRESENT: Spare bulb
LUCKY NUMBER: 83
HUMAN HERO: Matt Hayes
MOST LIKELY TO SAY: 'I'm going to lamp you.'
LEAST LIKELY TO SAY: 'Can't see a thing?'
BEST SERVED: With a light dressing! (Geddit?!?!!?)

MY INTERVIEW

ME: **My, you're a strange one.**
ANGLERFISH: *You can talk!*
ME: **What's so strange about me?!**
ANGLERFISH: *Look at you with your weird arms and legs!*
ME: **At least I don't have an Anglepoise lamp on my nose!**
ANGLERFISH: *Neither do I!*
ME: **Yes, you do!** [HANDS ANGLERFISH A MIRROR]
ANGLERFISH: *Oh my word, you're right! How did that get there?*
ME: **Evolution, I'd imagine.**
ANGLERFISH: *So you're suggesting that this device evolved on my nose? That the predatory instincts of my species could be served no better than by having a source of light on our noses?*
ME: **Hmm.**
ANGLERFISH: *I'm going to look this up in a proper book later.*
ME: **Feel free.**
ANGLERFISH: *I will.*
ME: **Be my guest.**

MY MONGOLIAN FISHING TRIP, 2002

When Sandra bought me a one-way ticket to Outer Mongolia for Christmas 2001, I did wonder about her motivations.

'Why Outer Mongolia?' I asked.

'*Er,*' she replied, and started phoning friends to arrange a series of parties in my absence. '*You wouldn't want me to be lonely while you're away,*' she explained.

'No, dear... But why only a one-way ticket?' I persisted.

'*I couldn't afford the return flight,*' she said.

Which seemed reasonable until I wondered aloud, '**Then why not buy me a return ticket to somewhere half as expensive?**'

Sandra said she had to put the turkey in the oven.

FISHY FACTS by DB Hartley

9 When a person catches 'crabs', these are actual crabs with pincers and everything! As you can imagine this can be quite a painful condition. At least the cure is simple: serve simply with freshly baked, crusty brown bread and a slice of lemon. Yum!

10 If you ever take a catfish home with you, you'll rapidly find out where the name comes from. In next to no time, they'll be running up the curtains, rubbing themselves against your legs and they can even be trained to defecate in the litter tray. Strangely, dogfish have never been known to fetch sticks or to show any of the attributes of our tail-wagging land friends.

Undeterred, I did some internet research on Mongolia's fishing opportunities and was stunned to find that it is home to the world's largest salmon, the tiamen. The world record specimen weighs in at over 200 pounds and so vast are these beasts that they eat actual mice and small rodents. Mongolians call it the 'river wolf'. Right, I thought, I'm going to catch me a tiamen!

Alongside my usual fishing tackle I packed our pet mouse, Mr Scruff. I can talk to mice as well as fish, and I explained to him that I was taking him on a cheese-tasting tour of Outer Mongolia. I didn't mention the tiamen. He seemed to swallow my story.

Come day one of the holiday, we're at a riverbank and I'm wrapping Mr Scruff in nylon with a hook on the end, and I can tell he's becoming suspicious because he starts asking about cheese.

> *'What sort of cheese do they have in Mongolia?'* and *'Surely there aren't any cheese shops on a riverbank?'* Whiny stuff.

Then I lob him in the fast-flowing river.

I am on tenterhooks. This is my big chance. How long before that first tiamen takes and I break the world Mongolian salmon record?

Some while later I still haven't had a bite and become a little suspicious. I follow my fly line with my eyes and realize that it has played out across the entire width of the river and continues into the far bank! I try reeling in, but the line will not budge.

Cursing Mr Scruff, I wade out, across the river and on to dry land on the other side, all the while following my line. A few yards in, I can see why I could not reel in – the line has been wrapped around a tree. Eventually, I come upon this little scene…

Mr Scruff had found some friends who were throwing a cheese and wine party!

> **'Why you little…!'** I exclaimed.
> *'Have you any idea how cold that water is?'* went Mr Scruff,
> through a mouthful of what looked like gorgonzola, holding a
> very small glass of chianti in his other paw.
> **'I just waded through it, didn't I?'**
> *'Yes, but you've got boots on!'* he protested.

Then all the other mice pitched in, but I couldn't understand them because they were speaking Mongolian. However from their tone I could tell they were irate. That's when the pangs of guilt kicked in. What had I been thinking? Dragging the family mouse to Outer Mongolia under false pretences, only to use him as bait? Despicable.

I decided there and then that landing the world's biggest tiamen meant nothing compared with my duty of care to Mr Scruff, and that we should return home immediately.

It was only when we arrived back at the airport that I remembered I didn't have a return ticket.

> *'That's OK,'* said the airport official. *'We're very low on
> electricity and can use your mouse friend here to turn the wheel
> that powers our dynamo.'*

'How long will it take him to work off the cost of my air ticket?' I asked.

'About three weeks,' said the official.

You should have seen the look that Mr Scruff gave me.

IN HIS DREAMS: MR SCRUFF ADMINISTERS JUSTICE FOR RODENTS

MY BRILLIANT IDEAS

No. 2

Bertie Big Mouth Bass

This one is a cracker! Amaze your friends and neighbours! Show them just what a devastatingly sophisticated sense of humour you possess! They'll laugh, they'll cry, they'll be enchanted – they'll want one! Of that, I guarantee you!

I came up with this idea one day when I landed a decent-sized bass and thought how comical it would be if I put a plastic bass on a wall and got it to sing a song. (Often the best ideas are the most obvious ones.) I dashed home to my workshop… Some 17 seconds later I had come up with a prototype, using the exoskeleton of a Terminator and some snot. Now I just had to make it sing. But which song? Which song?

Then it hit me. What better than a really crappy version of 'Take Me to the River'– geddit?!?! – written by Al Green and covered by Talking Heads?! That should make Al turn in his grave [HE ISN'T DEAD – ED.] and make David Byrne pull his own ears off using a pair of rusty pliers! And so it came to pass…

Before I hung Bertie Big Mouth on my wall, I had one friend. After, I had 100!

Soon, we were having Bertie Big Mouth parties, where everyone came dressed as bass and we'd hit that button over and over again, hearing old Bertie sing.

'TAKE ME TO THE RIVER!
DROP ME IN THE WATER!'

He's a fish – singing about being taken to a river! It just works!

Next thing you know, there's a Bertie on *The Sopranos*. Even the Queen of England has one!

After that I made countless versions of the same thing. Larry Loudmouth Lobster, Jaws Jaggedmouth Jaws, Tommy Troutmouth Trout, Colin Can-Anyone-Think-of-a-Word-Beginning-With-C Carp, etc., etc.

Did the joke wear thin? As gossamer. Gradually all my new friends drifted away and I lost some of the old ones, until it was just me and the wife again. I ritually burned all my Bertie Big Mouths and nowadays if I see one I puke spontaneously and stuff my head in the bucket.

You see anyone with a Bertie Big Mouth, still chuckling away, they're likeliest the bluntest tool in the box. But it was fun while it lasted!

HOW TO TICKLE A TROUT

Some consider it to be a myth that the stealthy and patient wader can actually tickle a trout. (By which I mean creeping up on said fish, tickling its tummy until it is lulled into a false sense of security, then scooping it on to dry land.)

Well, it isn't a myth and I know because I have achieved the feat. And without even getting in the water! All you will need is a megaphone; stand on the bank and tell the following jokes:

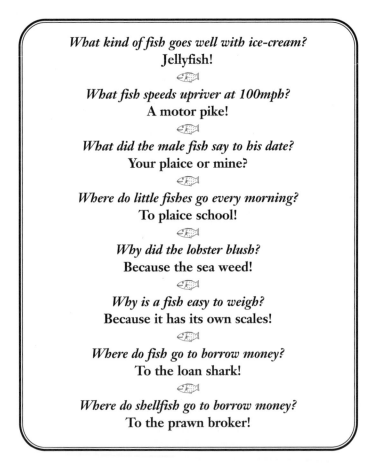

What kind of fish goes well with ice-cream?
Jellyfish!

What fish speeds upriver at 100mph?
A motor pike!

What did the male fish say to his date?
Your plaice or mine?

Where do little fishes go every morning?
To plaice school!

Why did the lobster blush?
Because the sea weed!

Why is a fish easy to weigh?
Because it has its own scales!

Where do fish go to borrow money?
To the loan shark!

Where do shellfish go to borrow money?
To the prawn broker!

So bad are the above that any self-respecting trout in the area will throw itself on to dry land, committing hara kiri, just to escape the awfulness. (I'll admit, I was tempted to throw myself into the water, too.)

And they said it couldn't be done!

YOUR SON'S FIRST FISHING TRIP*

(* THIS CAN ALSO WORK WITH DAUGHTERS, BUT IS LESS FOOLPROOF,
ESPECIALLY IF THE WIFE GETS TO HER FIRST.)

I t is the greatest day in the keen angler's life when their son grows old enough to be taken on his first fishing trip. I know it was mine.

Sandra and I have just the one child – a boy, hurrah! – whose name is Joe. I watched him grow and grow and grow and every night, at bedtime, I'd sit beside his bed and tell him true tales of my fishing exploits. Like the time I saved a sleepy lakeside town by catching the giant catfish that had been terrorizing the community every full moon.

Anyway, Joe grew and grew and grew and finally I decided he was old enough to be taken on his first fishing trip.

> **'You're going to enjoy this!'** I told him. **'Today signals the beginning of a lifetime of pleasure and adventure.'**
> *'But Dad, I'm only 18 months old,'* he protested.
> I waved his protestation away with a **'Pshaw!'**
> **'If you're old enough to eat rusks, you're old enough to fish!'** I assured him.

And off we went, to one of my favourite lakes: small enough for the beginner, yet well enough stocked that we were likely to catch something. This is the key, on any first fishing trip when the child is young:

YOU HAVE TO CATCH SOMETHING

I gave Joe the basics, as I saw them:

- How to set up his rod and reel
- How to tie a knot
- Which hook to choose
- Which bait to use
- How to gauge the conditions
- Where the fish are likely to be
- How to cast
- How to adjust the float length
- How a swim-feeder works
- When ledgering might be preferable
- The breeding habits of the tench
- How a fish's digestive system works
- The effect of the Trade Winds on the polar ice cap
- Einstein's theory of relativity
- Advanced molecular biology
- How to wear a hat

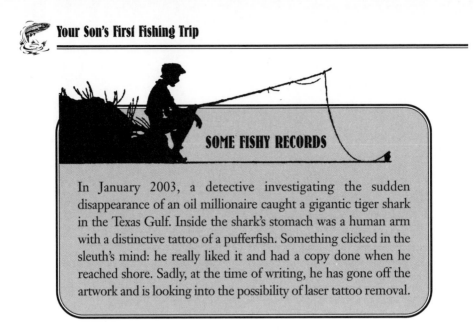

SOME FISHY RECORDS

In January 2003, a detective investigating the sudden disappearance of an oil millionaire caught a gigantic tiger shark in the Texas Gulf. Inside the shark's stomach was a human arm with a distinctive tattoo of a pufferfish. Something clicked in the sleuth's mind: he really liked it and had a copy done when he reached shore. Sadly, at the time of writing, he has gone off the artwork and is looking into the possibility of laser tattoo removal.

And we were ready! Was Joe excited? No. He told me he was tired and asked for a sandwich, and when I refused he started crying! The ingrate!

Eventually, after several sandwiches and some cola, while I became increasingly impatient, Joe declared that he was ready to fish. And we were off. It was my dream – and his! – coming true at last!

And you know, we fished most all day with nary a bite. Joe became increasingly restless while I became increasingly desperate. As I stated above:

YOU HAVE TO CATCH SOMETHING

And finally it happened! Strike! Reel-reel-reel, net-net-net – a fish! Joe's very first! And would you know it, it was a perch, just as my very first fish had been, all those years ago with my own Dad. Except mine was bigger.

Joe was elated. Job done! (As expected.) Bursting to tell Mum the exciting news, we climbed back into the car to head for home. Joe's breathless last words at the end of his very first fishing trip were:

> *'Dad, next time, will I be able to hold the rod at all?'*
> **'Course you will, son, course you will.'**

DUCK! (OR CAN FISH SEE YOU?)

I have already recounted, in this estimable tome, my experiments into the auditory faculties of fish (my conclusion being that there are none: that the average fish is deaf, that it would register not a blip on the Oh-Yes-I-Heard-That! scale if you were to suspend it among the bells of Big Ben and ring them as if war had broken out). However, there is another, possibly more significant, quandary for the angler: can fish see you?

All that walking along while crouching down, or hiding among weeds as if one is expecting incoming mortar fire. Is all that really necessary? Once again I have conducted some experiments which are scientifically watertight...

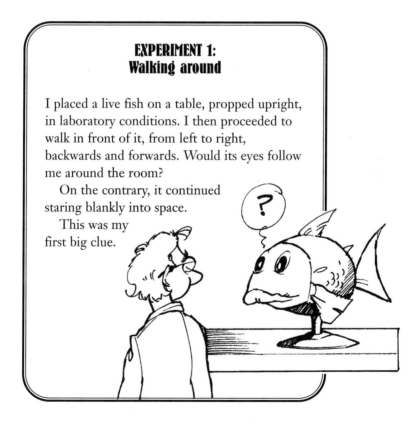

EXPERIMENT 1:
Walking around

I placed a live fish on a table, propped upright, in laboratory conditions. I then proceeded to walk in front of it, from left to right, backwards and forwards. Would its eyes follow me around the room?

On the contrary, it continued staring blankly into space.

This was my first big clue.

EXPERIMENT 2:
Dilation of pupils

The pupil of an eye should dilate to gain focus, when it encounters movement. This being the case, I loomed towards the fish and monitored any change in its pupil diameter. There was none. Then I wondered what that smell was and realized, as had happened in my previous experiment, that the fish had passed on. Again I replaced the subject with a new, far flappier fish, and repeated.

Still nothing.

This was my second big clue.

FISHY FACTS by DB Hartley

11 Ever wondered about the marvellous camouflaging abilities of the cuttlefish? I know I have. One moment it's one colour, the next it has flitted on and changed its skin tones to fit in with its new background. Amazing. But how does it do that? Remember Pablo Picasso? You think he's dead, don't you? Well, he's not. He moved underwater and now makes a living painting cuttlefish very quickly every time they move. (Which is why some cuttlefish seem to have eyes in funny places, and boobs.)

12 A middle-aged goldfish called Wolfram escaped from his bowl and decided to strike out across the English Channel for a new life in France. Tragically, he couldn't break the habit of a lifetime and, after swimming round in small circles for nine hours, gave up with the port of Dover still 100 yards to his left.

EXPERIMENT 3:
Mallet Test

If I am attacked with a mallet, I will look to see where the attack is coming from. Stands to reason. Therefore I attacked the subject from behind with a mallet.
Did it look around? No it did not. Indeed, when I laid it under a grill shortly afterwards, it did not seem in the least bit curious about the source of the heat.

This was my final big clue.

I can therefore scientifically, categorically state:

FISH CANNOT SEE YOU.

(Still it looks swish and professional stalking along a river bank ducking a lot, so go ahead and do it anyway. I know I do.)

MY BRILLIANT IDEAS

No. 3

Fish Attractors

It is one of the Holy Grails of angling to find a way to attract fish towards one's bait. Groundbaiting is one obvious method, and I have seen wacky electronic Sonic Fish Caller devices, which are supposed to emit a frequency that attracts fish. But I have another idea…

All fish look for a mate, it's in their DNA, as it is in ours. So what do we look for in a mate? My idea takes that question and applies it to fish. I have made two prototypes, one to attract male fish and one to attract female fish.

These are my plaster-cast prototypes, each designed to attract the opposite gender. You plant them on the bottom of a lake or river and then cast towards that area.

Males look for shapely females who might be open to their advances. Females, however, are more nurturing, looking for a caring partner. So I came up with these designs:

As I said, these are only prototypes and I am looking for a partner company to join with me to create thousands of these fish attractors for the marketplace. Please let me know if you're up for it…?

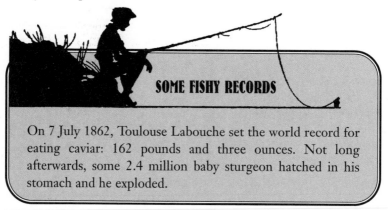

SOME FISHY RECORDS

On 7 July 1862, Toulouse Labouche set the world record for eating caviar: 162 pounds and three ounces. Not long afterwards, some 2.4 million baby sturgeon hatched in his stomach and he exploded.

THE COUNTRYSIDE CODE

As an angler, you'll be traipsing around a lot of countryside and plenty of public rights of way. So it's important to understand – and use – the Countryside Code, to respect the environment. Here it is:

① Country folk can be pretty weird.

② Well, you would be too if you only had a haystack, two pigs and a duck for company.

③ Some of them drive big tractors.

④ Not because they're doing any work, but so they can catch huge queues of traffic behind them and make everyone travel at 1mph.

⑤ Cows blowing off are making the polar ice caps disappear.

⑥ One day all the penguins will be dead. Blame the cows for that too.

⑦ Always close gates behind you.

⑧ One can only assume that pigs blow off too, but no one mentions them. Perhaps they hold it in?

⑨ In which case it's quite surprising that pigs don't fly. Some do, or so they say.

⑩ Always keep dogs under control.

⑪ Country folk are trigger-happy and will shoot practically anything that moves.

⑫ If you see a country person, put your hands in the air and say, 'I surrender' loudly and clearly just in case.

PIGS MIGHT FLY

⑬ Don't pick the wild flowers.

⑭ Unless they're very pretty.

⑮ Don't start fires.

⑯ Unless you're cold.

⑰ Country people always speak while chewing on a stalk of grass or corn. That's why you can never understand them.

⑱ So if one tries to talk to you just nod, say, 'Yes,' and laugh for no reason a few times. But keep walking.

⑲ Oooh, and don't drop litter.

⑳ (Just because 20 feels like a rounder number than 19.)

EXTREME FISHING

Spot of spear fishing among barracuda on a coral reef? Crack at the old hammerhead shark? Hovering around in a helicopter before dropping in on an unspoilt mountain lake several thousand feet above sea level?

Call those Extreme Fishing? Nah – this is Extreme Fishing...

1 Riding around on the back of a great white shark, wearing a suit and hat made from desiccated lamb chops, trailing a line behind you in the hope of catching whatever it is that's bonkers enough to prey on great whites

2 Surfing on an ironing board at the top of Niagara Falls, casting a line into the angriest white water, while being studied with great interest by a salivating vulture, drifting in the thermals 100 feet above your head

3 Hovering precariously above a bubbling pool of piranha in the Amazon, using children's helium balloons which are being popped one by one by inquisitive hummingbirds, with your big toe as bait since you forgot your fishing gear

4 Taunting a giant squid by suggesting you've seen bigger squid elsewhere, until it snaps at you and swallows you, then living in its throat with your head and arms at the entrance of its gob, pinching and eating anything it catches for breakfast, chuckling as you do so

FISHY FISH

Flying Fish

No. 5

NAME: **Flying fish**
LATIN NAME: *Weeeeeeee lookatmeus!*
ENVIRONMENT: **Far out to sea**

PROFILE

MOST LIKELY FOUND: Tinkering in a workshop
TEMPERAMENT: Easily pleased
FAVOURITE TV SHOW: *Airwolf*
FAVOURITE BOOK: *Now That's What I Call Flying* by the Wright Brothers
IDEAL BIRTHDAY PRESENT: Airline ticket
LUCKY NUMBER: 23
HUMAN HERO: Chuck Yeager
MOST LIKELY TO SAY: 'Weeeeeeeeeee!'
LEAST LIKELY TO SAY: 'Now, would you call that flying or jumping?'
BEST SERVED WITH: Fresh fruit salad

MY INTERVIEW

ME: **Could I just stop you for a second?**
FLYING FISH: *Weeeeee!*
ME: **If I could just have a quick word...**
FLYING FISH: *Weeeeee!*
ME: **Excuse me...**
FLYING FISH: *Look at me!*
ME: **I am doing.**
FLYING FISH: *I'm flying!*
ME: **Well...**
FLYING FISH: *What do you mean, 'Well...'?*
ME: **It's not really flying, is it?**
FLYING FISH: *It is!*
ME: **No it's not. It's more of a quite-long jump.**
FLYING FISH: *How dare you!*
ME: **But it's true!**
FLYING FISH: *It's not!*
ME: **All right then, fly to India.**
FLYING FISH: *Er.*

FISH IN THE MOVIES

Fish have starred in movies since the beginning of the movie business. They have everything a director could want: star quality, their own costume, sex appeal. [SEX APPEAL?! – ED.] So here, for your delectation, are just a few of the most memorable fish-studded epics. [YOU MEAN: HERE ARE THE ONLY ONES YOU COULD THINK OF? – ED.]

Jaws

What's it about? A great white shark terrorizes the tourist beach of a small town, while a series of stars whose names begin with R – Robert Shaw, Roy Scheider, Richard Dreyfuss – try to kill it. I bet if my name had been Rim instead of Jim, Spielberg would have given me a starring role too. [RIM? – ED.]

Is the fish the star? There's a clue in the title.

The fish's best line: *'Crunch, munch, belch.'*

Would you be able to catch that fish? I don't think so!

Would I be able to catch that fish? Possibly. Though even I'd be wary.

MY RATING (OUT OF 5): 🐟🐟🐟🐟🐟

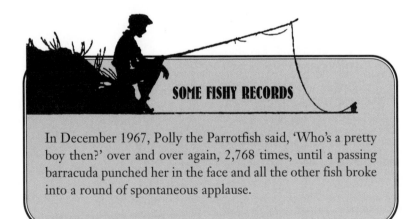

SOME FISHY RECORDS

In December 1967, Polly the Parrotfish said, 'Who's a pretty boy then?' over and over again, 2,768 times, until a passing barracuda punched her in the face and all the other fish broke into a round of spontaneous applause.

On Golden Pond

What's it about? An old man (Henry Fonda) attempts to catch a legendarily large trout (Walter) in his local lake (Golden Pond)… At least that should have been the focus. Instead it sidetracks into relationships. Snore. How does grouchy Fonda get on with his wife (Katharine Hepburn) and daughter (Jane Fonda)? Who cares?

Is the fish the star? No!

The fish's best line: *'Would you please stop nattering on and on about each other and try to catch me?'*

Would you be able to catch that fish? No.

Would I be able to catch that fish? Yes.

MY RATING: 🐟

A Fish Called Wanda

What's it about? Robbery and betrayal as John Cleese, Michael Palin and Kevin Kline all jockey for the amorous attentions of Jamie Lee Curtis. Both Curtis's character and the titular fish – Palin's tropical-fish pet – are both named Wanda, which is unnecessary and very confusing. But I know which Wanda I prefer. [I HAVE A TERRIBLE FEELING YOU DON'T MEAN LEE CURTIS – ED.]

Is the fish the star? Given that it ends up eaten by Kline and takes no part in the robbery, no. A wasted opportunity.

The fish's best line: *'But I'm not edib…'*

Would you be able to catch that fish? Given that it's in a tank, possibly.

Would I be able to catch that fish? Wouldn't bother, too small.

MY RATING: 🐟🐟

A River Runs Through It

What's it about? Craig Sheffer and Brad Pitt are brothers (in the film), one saintly, the other wayward. They go fly fishing but talk too much while doing so, instead of concentrating on the trout.

Is the fish the star? Hardly, though this is of more interest than *On Golden Pond*.

The fishes' best lines: *'I'm going to be caught by that lovely Brad Pitt!' 'No, you aren't, I am!'*

Would you be able to catch that fish? No.

Would I be able to catch that fish? Yes.

MY RATING: 🐟🐟🐟

Finding Nemo

What's it about? A young clownfish (Nemo) becomes separated from his father (Marlin). Marlin and Dory (a regal tang – that's another tropical fish, not a tasty royal person) go in search of the youngster, encountering a wild and

colourful cast of undersea creatures during their quest.

Is the fish the star? Every star is a fish! All the fish are stars! This is how all films should be made! [YOU DO REALIZE THEY AREN'T REAL? – ED.]

The fishes' best lines: Every line's a gem.

Would you be able to catch that fish? No.

Would I be able to catch that fish? Yes.

MY RATING: 🐟 🐟 🐟 🐟

Big Fish

What's it about? A big fish – what did you think it would be about? [WELL, THERE'S A BIT MORE TO IT THAN THAT. YOU HAVEN'T MENTIONED ALBERT FINNEY OR EWAN MCGREGOR – ED.]

Is the fish the star? The film's called *Big Fish*, isn't it? [YES, BUT THE STORY'S ALLEGORICAL – ED.] Is it?

The fish's best line: Now, let me think… [HAVE YOU EVEN SEEN THE MOVIE? – ED.]

I'm sorry, I can't work under these conditions.

OTHER BOX OFFICE SMASHES

FIELD OF BREAMS	CITY OF COD	STARFISH WARS
BEVERLY HILLS CARP	THE DA VINCI COD	THE SWORDFISH AND
WHITEBAIT CAN'T	THE CODFATHER	THE STONE
JUMP	ANCHOVY'S ASHES	A-PIKE-ALYPSE NOW
THE SEAHORSE	TROUT OF AFRICA	BLACK NEWT-Y
WHISPERER	PRAWN OF THE DEAD	ORCA THE LINE
ANEMONE OF	MANATEE ON FIRE	ERIN BROCKAFISH
THE SKATE	SOME PIKE IT HOT	FILLET-DELPHIA
GENTLEMEN PREFER	GOOD MORNING	GUNFIGHT AT THE
PONDS	VIET-CLAM	OK CORAL

WHY ANGLERS ARE WEIRD

Now, there's nothing wrong with an artificial fly. Some can be quite dramatic, works of art almost. Aesthetically pleasing, you might say. Ditto the artificial lure. So you're thinking: What's he on about? Why on earth does using bait make me weird? Let me enlighten you with a quick illustration...

WHAT NORMAL PEOPLE DO WITH MAGGOTS	WHAT ANGLERS DO WITH MAGGOTS
Run away from them, dry-heaving with revulsion.	**Stare at them lovingly and store them in the fridge.**

Next thing you know, doddery Aunt Ada, the one with the iffy eyesight, has raided the refrigerator at night, felt for the Tupperware container and thought to herself: Hehe, this'll do. Alerted by the commotion, you've leapt downstairs in your jim-jams, switched on the kitchen light, and there she is on the floor, shrieking, with a mouthful of dyed grubs and the occasional half-eaten bluebottle. It ain't pretty.

PUT SIMPLY,
THIS IS WRONG:

To be fair, it gets worse. Lugworms!?! Ragworms!??!?!

Ragworms look like the demon spawn of a millipede and the Toxic Avenger. Who'd go near one, let alone pick one up and thread it on to a big hook, until ragworm guts ran over their fingers?

Oh, you would.

See?

But the very worst bait of all is that concocted by the bait fetishists. You know them. Those anglers who mix their own 'recipes', like demented warlocks.

> [READ THE FOLLOWING SENTENCE TO YOURSELF IN A DEMENTED-WARLOCK VOICE] 'EYE OF TOAD AND WING OF BAT, ROTTEN FISH MIXED UP WITH THAT; ADD CHICKEN GUTS AND MIX BY HAND; AND SOON THE BIGGEST FISH I'LL LAND [NOW REVERT TO NORMAL VOICE]… or failing that I'll have no friends and strangers will run away from me holding their noses.

The things we anglers do for love.

FISHY FACTS by DB Hartley

People often ask me, 'Hey, DB, how come you know next to nothing about fishing facts, yet you're writing about fishing facts for a highly respected book about fishing which contains nothing but solid fact and not one single iota of rank stupidity?' And I say to them, 'Seventh Floor, Lingerie Department,' which throws them for just long enough for me to run away and hide behind a very large turnip.

ONE FOR THOSE YOU LEAVE BEHIND

All this fabulous and factually correct info on fishing for you, yet nothing on offer for your angling-averse partner? It doesn't seem right to forget about them – I know I always set aside time to think about the wife. Generally around 11.42 am every Wednesday. I'm joking, of course!

So let's spare our partners a thought, reward them for their patience, understanding and support. You've had your How Hooked Are You? quiz. Now here's a How Unhooked Are You? quiz for them. Same rules apply.

QUESTION 1

Your partner says they're off out fishing yet again. What is your first thought?

A) [ENTIRELY UNPRINTABLE]
B) 'What a sad [REMAINDER UNPRINTABLE]'
C) 'At least it's only every weekend. And Christmas Day, Boxing Day and miscellaneous public holidays. And, come to think of it, our anniversary… [REMAINDER UNPRINTABLE]'
D) 'Ah, let them have their fun'

QUESTION 2

While your partner is out fishing, how do you tend to occupy your time?

A) By sleeping with the next-door neighbour
B) By cutting random holes out of their clothing using a big pair of scissors
C) By tapping your foot impatiently while watching *Psycho*
D) 'There's always a dinner to prepare, whether it goes cold or not. It's the thought that counts'

QUESTION 3

Your partner suggests that you join them on a fishing trip. 'Who knows, you might even enjoy yourself?' they add wishfully.

A) 'I'd enjoy myself more if someone cut off my feet, Sellotaped one over each eye and declared that they made an attractive novelty pair of horn-rimmed spectacles'

B) 'I'd enjoy myself more if someone asked me to watch over their pet walnut named Nicholas until they returned – and then went missing for 14 years'

C) 'You must be joking!'

D) 'Why not! I'd like that very much!'

QUESTION 4

Opening a rarely used cupboard, a series of carrier bags fall out. They're full of recently purchased fishing tackle which your partner has tried to hide from you. What do you do?

A) Ram it item by item [REMAINDER UNPRINTABLE]
B) Put the lot on a bonfire then invite your partner outside to warm their hands, and wait gleefully while their expression begins to change
C) Confront them, shouting. Force them to take it all back for a refund.
D) Take a deep interest and ask what each item does, while remaining wide awake

QUESTION 5

Your partner returns home delighted after a successful sea-fishing trip, and slaps on the kitchen table what they claim to be 'a near-record whiting!' How do you react?

A) Pick it up and recreate as best you can – accuracy isn't the point – Monty Python's fish-slapping dance, wishing only that the whiting were of actual record size
B) Lob it in the bin and file for divorce
C) Tell them that if they're so pleased with it, they can eat it. Then sit and watch them do so, having tied them to a chair
D) Warm the oven and begin filleting

QUESTION 6

Your partner decides it's time to take your young child on their first-ever fishing trip. Clearly a desperate attempt at indoctrination, what do you do? There's a chance it might be successful...

A) While your partner's away, you stick *Jaws* in the DVD player and hope aloud that no one catches a fish that big

B) Puncture all the tyres on the car and swear that badgers did it during the night

C) Howl 'Nooooooooooooooooooooooooooooooo', which goes on for ages, then beat your fists against the floor, weeping uncontrollably

D) 'What a fabulous idea, darling! I do hope you have a lovely time. Here, I've packed some sandwiches'

QUESTION 7

What do you think your partner looks like, kitted out in their full fishing regalia?

A) A loser
B) Pffffffffffffttttttt!
C) Not exactly trendy
D) Rather lovely

QUESTION 8

Out drinking one evening, a good friend suddenly lets rip, declaring that, 'Your partner is a no-good, selfish, boring, conniving, fish-obsessed waste of a human being'. What do you do?

A) Demand to know whether they're having an affair, as the only person to know them as well as that is you

B) Pat them on the back and buy them another drink

C) After the initial shock, you begin to agree

D) Threaten to sue for slander

QUESTION 9

Your partner announces that they have invited their fishing friends round for a drinks party. How do you react?

A) You burn the house down

B) Just as the 'party' is getting started, you enter the lounge wearing an ice-hockey mask and jumpsuit, smilingly declaring you are Jason from the *Friday the 13th* series of movies. You refuse all requests to remove the mask and hover near guests until they become disturbed and leave

C) You suddenly find you have a prior engagement that evening – your toenails need cutting in the loft

D) You mingle with the party guests, hanging on their every fishing tale, and distributing nibbles

QUESTION 10

It's Christmas! On tenterhooks, you open the present from your partner to discover a Bertie Big Mouth Bass. Not only do they find the irony of you receiving a fish-related gift hilarious, they also find Bertie Big Mouth Bass hilarious. In your state of overwhelming fury, you cannot decide which is worse. But how do you seek revenge?

A) The following year you lie in wait for Santa Claus, knock him out cold with the Bertie Big Mouth and prop his unconscious form up at the foot of your partner's bed. When they wake up expectantly on Christmas morning, you tell them, 'You did this!'

B) When your partner falls asleep that night, you remove Bertie Big Mouth's mechanism and insert it into their snoring gob. When they wake up, they find themselves repeatedly singing a crappy version of 'Take Me to the River' while turning their head

C) The following year you give them a set of *Jerry Springer Show* DVDs

D) Kick them out of the house, invite some friends round for drinks and all point, laughing, while they shiver in the garden, begging to be let back in. Yay!

SCORING SYSTEM *If you answered:* A) Score 3 points B) Score 2 points C) Score 1 point D) Score 0 points *Now calculate your total*

RATINGS GUIDE 0–14 points – *Congratulations You are a saint* 15–29 points – *Hmmm! A little less 'you' time might be in order* 30 points – *Psycho! Makes me glad I met Sandra!*

SOME SILLY FISH NAMES

Read these with the same pleasure you give to the reading of a class register. These are all genuine names, by the way.

African lungfish
Alfonsino
Blenny
Broadband dogfish
Burrowing goby
California halibut
Crappie
Death Valley pupfish
Dottyback

Elasmobranch
Fathead sculpin
Fire bar danio
Flabby whalefish
Flagblenny
Garibaldi
Grunion
Grunt
Grunter

Gudgeon
Gulper
Gurnard
Haddock
Hagfish
Halibut
Hog sucker
Humuhumu-nukunuku-
    apua'a (SORRY ABOUT
    THAT ONE)
Jack Dempsey
John Dory
Kaluga
Ling
Longjaw mudsucker
Loosejaw
Louvar
Luderick
Madtom
Modoc sucker
Molly
Morwong
Mullet
Mummichog
Nibbler
Noodlefish
Oldwife

Orbicular batfish
Peter's elephantnose fish
Pilchard
Raccoon butterfly fish
Rasbora
Riffle dace
Rocket danio
Ronquil
Sarcastic fringehead
Scat
Sculpin
Scup
Snook
Tang
Tarpon
Tench
Tidewater goby
Tube-eye
Tube-snout
Turbot
Wahoo
Warty angler
Whiff
Zingel

HOW TO CAST A FLY

It's not easy learning to fly-cast, let me tell you. In my early days I had fly-hooks in my ears, up my nose, in trees, in my hat, in three ducks, one swan and a passing lemming, and in one terribly embarrassing incident, in the buttock of a lady who was walking behind me. Happily the lady in question was Sandra and I placated her with a pair of Ron Thompson neoprene chest waders.

The idea is to give the line momentum by false-casting, as it's called. Which largely involves one frantically whipping one's rod backwards and forwards, then landing the fly on the water amid a mass of fly-line loops and such cacophony that every trout in the country – and some neighbouring countries, if close enough – has swum for cover.

I once went fly fishing in Luxembourg and no one caught anything in Belgium, Holland, Germany or France for two days afterwards. I heard some fruity cursing, believe me, but at least I couldn't understand any of it. There's something to be said for not concentrating in school.

So let's forget about actual fly-casting and focus on some excellent options instead. Ignore the roll cast, the reverse cast and the double haul – try these:

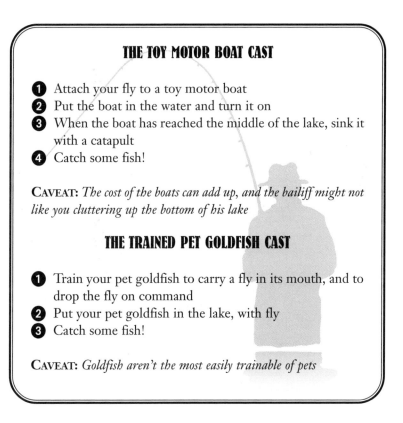

THE TOY MOTOR BOAT CAST

1. Attach your fly to a toy motor boat
2. Put the boat in the water and turn it on
3. When the boat has reached the middle of the lake, sink it with a catapult
4. Catch some fish!

CAVEAT: *The cost of the boats can add up, and the bailiff might not like you cluttering up the bottom of his lake*

THE TRAINED PET GOLDFISH CAST

1. Train your pet goldfish to carry a fly in its mouth, and to drop the fly on command
2. Put your pet goldfish in the lake, with fly
3. Catch some fish!

CAVEAT: *Goldfish aren't the most easily trainable of pets*

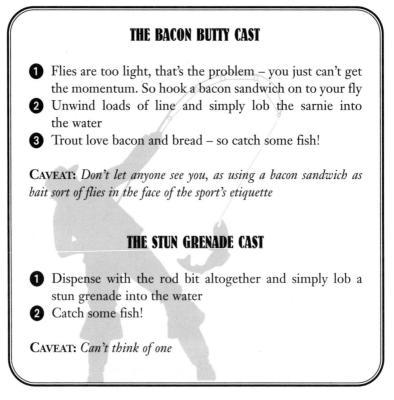

THE BACON BUTTY CAST

1 Flies are too light, that's the problem – you just can't get the momentum. So hook a bacon sandwich on to your fly

2 Unwind loads of line and simply lob the sarnie into the water

3 Trout love bacon and bread – so catch some fish!

CAVEAT: *Don't let anyone see you, as using a bacon sandwich as bait sort of flies in the face of the sport's etiquette*

THE STUN GRENADE CAST

1 Dispense with the rod bit altogether and simply lob a stun grenade into the water

2 Catch some fish!

CAVEAT: *Can't think of one*

WHAT THE &%$* IS THAT?!

There are perhaps thousands of sea creatures that remain undiscovered by we humans, lying deep, deep down in trenches beneath the waves. Creatures like this one below:

I caught that while fishing off a boat in the North Sea, using a 50-pound line and a reel the size of a beer barrel. Imagine my shock when I hauled it on board! As it plopped on to the deck, it groaned a terrible groan that sounded like,

'IFYOUTHINKI'MWEIRDWAITTILLYOUSEEMYDAD.'

Then it tried to eat the side of the boat.

The Society for the Identification of Weird New Fishes and Undersea Critters credited me with the creature's discovery and it's currently stuffed in a cabinet at the Museum of Curiosities. They said I could name it after myself, but who wants something like that named after them? So I called it Sandra, since it bears more than a passing resemblance. (I HAVEN'T TOLD HER YET.)

SOME FISHWIVES' TALES

Some fishwives, yesterday

Fishwives are women who are married to fish. The clue's in the name. They are therefore quite possibly shortsighted and most definitely poor judges of character.

Since fish generally open and close their mouths silently, perhaps eating the odd insect, they aren't great company. Thus do fishwives gossip to each other all day, until they are forced to make things up for fear of their conversation becoming repetitive. For this reason they are not to be trusted.

Need proof? Let's look at some fishwives' tales...

FISHWIFE TALE ❶

'I just bought a cabbage and it had arms and legs and it spoke to me.'

FISHWIFE TALE ❷

'Some people say that William Shakespeare didn't write all them plays and that's right. My husband, who is a chub, wrote them.'

FISHWIFE TALE ❸

'I wished I was dead, I really did. And then I was dead and then I came back to life and I was reincarnated as a squirrel. So the next time you see a squirrel, that's me. It is.'

FISHWIFE TALE ❹

'It's bad luck to take a banana on a fishing boat. Why? Er. Because mischievous little people live in bananas and when night falls they peel the bananas and slaughter the crew with pickaxes, then burn the boat down.'

FISHWIFE TALE ❺

'So I said to Ethel, and then she said to me, and well I never did! And you wouldn't believe it! I know! Oooh, I've warned them before! I did, didn't I? I know! And did you see Cedric? He wasn't! He was! I know! Well, if ask me...'

[YES, THAT'S ENOUGH FISHWIVES' TALES – ED.]

BENSON

You may have heard about the common carp named Benson, who died in Bluebell Lakes, Peterborough, England, weighing almost 65 pounds. She'd been round the block a few times. During 14 years in the lake, she was caught on 63 separate occasions. I spoke to Benson shortly before her untimely demise.

ME: **Benson, hello.**
BENSON: *Hello.*
ME: **You're said to be the most famous carp in Britain. How do you feel about that?**
BENSON: *Got any nuts? I'm starving.*
ME: **Don't you know that unprocessed nuts can be harmful to carp?**
BENSON: *Perhaps you didn't hear me. I said: I'm. Starving.*
ME: **Have you ever considered a diet?**
BENSON: *What are you, Weightwatchers?*
ME: **You do weigh 65 pounds.**
BENSON: *I'm big-boned!*
ME: **Your lake owner, Mr Bridgefoot, has been quoted as saying, 'If there were nuts [on offer], she would have eaten the lot. She was a greedy fish.'**
BENSON: *I can't help worrying more about his use of the past tense than the 'greedy' bit.*
ME: **Slip of the tongue.**
BENSON: *You wouldn't be making this interview up using information from a news report published shortly after my death in August 2009, and passing it off as having been conducted beforehand? It's enough to turn a fish to drink.*
ME: **You've been caught more than 60 times, I believe?**
BENSON: *Now that's something I'd like to talk about. Here, look at my lips...*
ME: **And?**
BENSON: *Look at 'em! Shot to pieces! You ever tried applying lipstick to lips that have been hooked upwards of 60 times, and they're pulling one way and you're trying to pull the other?*

ME: **No.**

BENSON: *You just try it!*

ME: **I'd rather not.**

BENSON: *See?!*

ME: **There's no need to get uptight.**

BENSON: *Uptight?! You want to try attracting the attentions of a gentleman carp when your lips look like two buns attacked by starlings!*

ME: **I assure you I don't.**

BENSON: *Have you any idea how paranoid it made me, wondering whether any single morsel of food I ate might be attached to a hook, and I'd have to go through all that dragged-to-the-bank rigmarole again?*

ME: **Judging by the size of you, you** somehow managed to get past it.

BENSON: *Then you're dragged up on to dry land, thinking here we go again, and there's some sweaty bloke heavy-breathing all over you, going, 'Oooh, quick, get the camera! Get the camera!' Forget the camera! Just put me back in the water, you moron!*

ME: **I don't...**

BENSON: *Then they're trying to lift me up, like I'm some kind of ceremonial jelly! Manhandling my bits and pieces, grubby fingers all over my lovely scales. It's so undignified!*

ME: **Would you like some lovely sweetcorn?**

BENSON: *Now you're talking! Gimme that! ... Hold on – there's a hook in this! THERE'S A HOOK IN THIS! You're actually trying to catch me during an interview! Are there no depths to which you won't stoop?*

ME: Cough.

MY MARTIAN FISHING TRIP

You know what my first thought was when I heard they'd discovered water on Mars? Yup. When's the first flight out – I'm gonna fish me that puppy! And so it was that I went fishing on Mars.

It was a pretty dull journey, I can tell you, so thank heavens for my maggots, which hatched into flies and I played games with them such as backgammon and ludo. Once they died I started to win, and luckily I'd packed some tinned sweetcorn so I'd still have some bait once I arrived on Mars.

Seven months and 36 million miles later – a noticeable trip – I landed on Mars and unpacked my rod. What would I catch? I took my place on the canal bank and waited.

Soon I had a beauty. This fish had scales and fins in all the right places but weighed next to nothing due to local gravity. It struck me that fish are the same the universe over. So I tonked it on the head and ate it – and very tasty it was too. A bit like pork, and rather bony. Then I realized I'd barbecued my numbed hand and was eating my own index finger! Ouch!

That was when I realized I'd had enough of Mars and its stupid fish, so I climbed back into my spacecraft and hit the button marked '*Head For Home, Good Buddy!*'

Seven months later, I was back home and being greeted like a returning hero – which I guess I was – by various of the world's top dignitaries. They wanted to give me a Nobel Prize but I was too tired and I said to them, 'Thanks but no thanks,' and they pinned the Nobel Prize on my back as I was leaving and [THAT'S ENOUGH OF YOUR MARTIAN FISHING TRIP – ED.]

THE WORST QUESTION IN THE WORLD

If you're a keen angler, you'll know the one. Those 'three little words'. Actually, one of the words is quite long and another's medium-sized, but 'three little words' sounded good. So. Anyone?

'CAUGHT ANYTHING YET?'

I should stress that said question only troubles people who haven't caught anything yet, which rarely includes me. Admittedly, it did the first couple of times I went fishing – so I do understand the pain – but after that I mastered the sport very quickly and it didn't bother me at all.

This is probably the ideal time to tell you about my third fishing trip. 'Impromptu' doesn't cover the half of it. I was 11 years old and Dad had stopped in a lay-by on the way to a new fishing lake, to stretch his legs. Bored, I got my fishing tackle out of the boot, set up my rod, popped a worm on the end and practised casting towards a puddle some 20 yards away.

'Plop!' – my worm lands in the puddle first time around. And to my great surprise, there's a take. I've only caught the world record mirror carp!

I know, I couldn't believe it either!

So.

'CAUGHT ANYTHING YET?'

Hurts, doesn't it? Because you haven't. You've been fishing for several hours with nary a nibble. And some git's come along and forced your inadequacy down your throat.

'CAUGHT ANYTHING YET?'

Your reply has to sound carefree.

'I'VE ONLY CAUGHT THE WORLD RECORD MIRROR CARP'

'No... Not yet! Hahahaha!'

A brazen mixture of honesty, wishful thinking and fake laughter. You sound like a single lady desperate for a husband. And now you know what's expected of you. You have no choice – you have to return the question. That's just etiquette. Go on, off you go...

'You?'

The worst part is that you know the answer already, because no one with a catch lighter than Satan's goody bag would invite the same question.

'Oh, since you ask,' they trill back, all breezy innocence. 'Yes, had a couple/few/load. Keep on in there!'

So what should you do in this situation? What's the best way to respond to the Worst Question in the World?

'Caught anything yet?'

I know I shouldn't be saying this, and it's certainly something I would never resort to, but perhaps you should consider lying? Or at least exaggerating a touch?

Let's see how that works.

EXAMPLE 1: EXAGGERATING

GIT: **Caught anything yet?**
YOU: *Yeah, couple of dozen. Whoppers, too.*
GIT: **Oh.**
[SLINKS OFF, MUTTERING TO SELF]

EXAMPLE 2: LYING

GIT: **Caught anything yet?**
YOU: *Nope. But then I only just got here because I've been sleeping with your wife/husband.*
GIT: **Why you...**

I think merely exaggerating might suffice.

BRILLIANT IDEAS

No. 4   Crane Fishing

Ever watched a crane in action and thought to yourself: You know, that looks exactly like a giant fishing rod? No, I thought you hadn't. It takes a special type of mind.

The way the crane arm swivels round, with the big hook on the end – it's like the crane driver is casting. So I thought to myself: I wonder whether I could fish with a crane? I'd catch the world's biggest monster fish if I could!

See – in principle a crane and a fishing rod are exactly the same. However, there was one obstacle: the hook on the crane was so large, I obliterated the first worms I tried to hang on it. They were way too small. So I realized: if my daring experiment was going to work, I needed to breed the world's first superworm!

But how?

I had to make some connections: superworm... Superman... superheroes... radiation! So I set to thinking. I would need:

 WORM TEST SUBJECT
SOME PLUTONIUM
RADIATION SUIT

Plutonium's easy enough to come by if you have the right contacts. I won't go into any details. Suffice to say that I got some. My suppliers threw in a radiation suit for free. And a fishing friend gave me half a dozen of the healthiest worms from his wormery. I was good to go!

However, I wasn't entirely sure how to mix the worms and the plutonium to create the desired effect, namely a worm large enough to fit on a crane hook. My first five experiments, conducted in the basement, involved the death of each worm and Sandra's hair falling out upstairs. She wasn't best pleased and neither was I. It left me with one worm. One last worm.

The scene was set for my final attempt to create the world's first superworm when Sandra (weakly) called me upstairs. The television was on, showing the local news.

> *'That's our street, isn't it?'* said Sandra.
> *'Hmm,'* I replied, nervously.
> *'Why are there people with Geiger counters wandering around outside?'* she asked.

That was the end of my experiments. I took the plutonium and the radiation suit back, buried the five worms, locked the basement door forever and the news crews went away. Even Sandra's hair grew back, which was a bonus. If it was a failed experiment, it was still a Brilliant Idea, which is why I include it here. And though I shall never go down into that basement again – too many bad memories – I do wonder about that final worm abandoned down there. I assume residual radioactivity consigned it to the same fate as the others. Let that be an end to the matter.

HOW COME WE CAN WATCH FISHING PROGRAMMES FOR HOURS ON END AND NEVER GET BORED?

It concerns me sometimes, too, in my more lucid moments. I could sit in front of the cable fishing shows for days on end, never blinking, until my body began to liquefy – as once happened. Had Sandra not reacted quickly and shoved my legs in the freezer, I might have had to store my feet in a pair of jugs.

So what is it about fishing shows? Why can we watch Rex Hunt/Bob James/Chris Yates/Steve Pennaz/Hank Parker/Matt Hayes/Bill Dance/John Anderson/Paul Young/etc. (delete/add as appropriate) forever and never get bored? At the end of the day, we're watching them catch fish, perhaps receiving a little tuition along the way, but generally watching them catch fish. And as Charlie Brown would so often say:

THAT'S IT!

I love watching people catch fish on television. Why? Because when I'm not fishing I'm at home – but I'd rather be fishing. And through the fishing shows I can fish vicariously. It's like I'm forever fishing, in my head. This can lead to problems in my relationship.

> SANDRA: *Do you like my nightie?*
> ME: **I prefer the lugworm.**
> SANDRA: *Are you daydreaming about fishing again?*
> ME: **I've caught a gurnard!**
> SANDRA: *I give up!*
> ME: [SNAPPING OUT OF IT] **Sorry, darling. Here, have a bag of ground bait.**
> SANDRA: *And a candlelit dinner?*
> ME: **That ground bait was £2.69!**

And somehow we muddle through.

WHAT FISH GET UP TO UNDERWATER

They're down there, we just can't see them. And just because we can't see them, that doesn't mean they aren't having a great time. So what do fish get up to underwater?

Consider this: ever wondered how we can tempt fish time and time again with a tasty worm, yet they never give it a second glance? Fish love worms, right? So what on earth can be going on down there that is preferable to chomping on that yummy invertebrate?

I'll tell you. Cinematic revenge... *Jaws* is still showing at most undersea cinemas.

TYING YOUR OWN ARTIFICIAL FLIES

Y ou'll need a good and varied box of flies if you're taking up fly fishing, and though individual flies don't tend to be too expensive, they do start to add up when bought in quantity. What a lot of keen types do is to tie their own. Personally, I tried and I was hopeless. [I'M SORRY? – ED.]

Why, what's the matter?
[WHAT YOU JUST SAID – ED.]
You've lost me.
[DID YOU USE THE WORDS 'I' AND 'HOPELESS' TOGETHER IN AN ANGLING-RELATED SENTENCE? – ED.]
I'm not altogether sure I follow your drift. Are you suggesting I'm not generally modest re my fishing capabilities?
[HAVE YOU READ THE REST OF THE BOOK? – ED.]
Strange chap. Anyway, I tried fly-tying and it wasn't for me.
[YOU MEAN YOU WERE RUBBISH AT IT? – ED.]
I wouldn't say I was rubbish...
[OH, GO ON, JUST FOR ME – ED.]
Well. I was... slightly... I was...
[RUBBISH? – ED.]
All right, if you wish, I was rubbish.
[AT SOMETHING TO DO WITH FISHING... – ED.]

Look, this is becoming tiresome for me, and I'm sure it's annoying the readers.

[NO IT ISN'T! – THE READERS.]

Very well. If it pleases you so very much, I shall explain why I wasn't great at fly-tying.

[YAY! – EVERYONE.]

I bought all the kit:

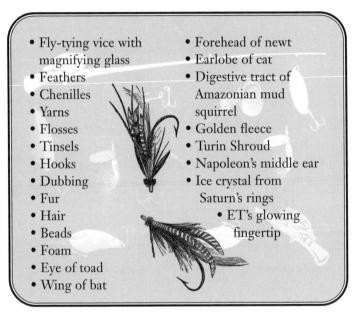

- Fly-tying vice with magnifying glass
- Feathers
- Chenilles
- Yarns
- Flosses
- Tinsels
- Hooks
- Dubbing
- Fur
- Hair
- Beads
- Foam
- Eye of toad
- Wing of bat
- Forehead of newt
- Earlobe of cat
- Digestive tract of Amazonian mud squirrel
- Golden fleece
- Turin Shroud
- Napoleon's middle ear
- Ice crystal from Saturn's rings
- ET's glowing fingertip

I could go on, but it would make me weep.

[PLEASE GO ON THEN – EVERYONE.]

The idea was that I would shell out in the short term to save in the long run. But do you have any idea how ridiculously fiddly it is to tie your own flies? Great, suddenly everyone stops interjecting. Then I'll tell you how ridiculously fiddly it was. Very. Very ridiculously fiddly.

[SO WHAT HAPPENED? – EVERYONE.]

Well, I increasingly lost my patience and got in a bit of a strop.
And, well, I started throwing things around. I went a bit mad.
Lost my cool and composure.

[AND? – EVERYONE.]

And Sandra came down and she said to me, *'Who's this? The Birdman of Alcatraz?'*

I'll thank you to keep the story to yourselves.

[OH, YOU CAN TRUST US, DON'T YOU WORRY – EVERYONE.]

FISHING – IT'S NOT ALL ABOUT
CATCHING FISH*
(* It is)

Other anglers have said to me, *'Jim, I don't go fishing purely to catch fish – if I do land something, that's merely a bonus. I go fishing because I love the tranquillity, the solitude and the feeling that I am at one with nature.'*

'And to get away from the wife!' I always add, and they don't laugh.

Can this really be the case, or are these people defeatists who aren't terribly good at fishing if they're honest with themselves? Surely the point of fishing is to catch fish and nothing else. Here follow some inanities they spout, and my responses…

THEM: *'Look, a moorhen! Isn't the bird life here wonderful?'*
ME: 'No, it isn't. I am not a birdwatcher – I wouldn't know a bird if you flew one into my face. I would think it was a very small aeroplane.'

THEM: *'These trees are so majestic, don't you think?'*
ME: 'No, I don't. I am not into trees – I mean, who is?'

THEM: *'One of the things I love most about fishing is the solitude.'*
ME: 'Then why don't you stop $&%!& talking!'

THEM: *'Oooh, look, a dragonfly!'*
ME: 'And?'

THEM: *'Doesn't the sky look amazing today?'*
ME: 'It looks to me as it normally looks. Like sky.'

THEM: *'Don't the clouds look amazing today?'*
ME: 'Look, I think I covered this one with "sky" (above)!'

THEM: *'What marvellous flowers, grasses and shrubs there are here!'*
ME: 'Shlowers, shrasses and shru... Hang on, that doesn't work.'

THEM: *'I adore the drifting sounds of nature!'*
Me: 'I can hear enough drifting sounds of nature from the comfort of my own armchair after a plate of beans.'

THEM: *'Ah, the wind in my hair, the...'*
ME: 'Don't even go there.'

THEM: *'How peaceful it is here!'*
ME: 'Peace is overrated – look what happened to John Lennon.'

Call me a curmudgeon, but I can't stand fishing small talk.

ALTERNATIVE FISHING METHODS

Did you know that fishermen in Japan and China use cormorants to catch their fish for them? It's terribly clever and requires the following:

- NO ROD
- NO REEL
- NO MOUNDS OF TACKLE
- NO FIDDLY KNOTS
- NO ABILITY TO CAST
- NO ICKY LIVE BAIT
- NO MYSTICAL SENSE OF ONENESS WITH NATURE
- NO EXAGGERATING
- NO BORING THE MISSUS
- NO WEARING OF A WAISTCOAT
- NO PATIENCE OF A SAINT
- NO WEEING INTO WADERS WHILE TRYING TO LOOK INNOCENT
- NOTHING

You simply need to be:

GOOD MATES WITH A CORMORANT

The bird dives under the water and grabs the fish in its beaks. A loose loop around its neck prevents it from swallowing the fish, which it takes back to the fisherman, who releases it into his pot. Couldn't be easier!

Those Chinese and Japanese chappies simply watched the cormorants in action and put two and two together. Fishing comes naturally to the bird, so harness that ability.

And it got me thinking. Aren't there other creatures out there that are far better at fishing than we humans, who might be used to help swell our catch bags? First I thought about the otter, but their mouths are only so big and I imagine they have terrible halitosis. If you're going to spend all that time training an animal, why settle for such a small return?

And I thought about the raccoon. But that's pretty much the same size as an otter, only stripier.

Or the beaver? Too flappy-tailed.

Then it hit me!

THE ANNUAL FISHING CLUB DINNER

Most days of the year, it suffices for customers to point a finger at the floating menu in Mad Luigi's fresh fish diner. This all changes when members of the Horsey Windpump angling club turn up for their annual dinner. Unfortunately, three minutes after the events shown in this picture, one of the members hooked a passing patrolman in the eye and everyone had to go home early via the local police station…

CAN YOU TRUST THE LOCALS?

I t is often said that the best way to learn about a lake or river that is alien to you is to ask the locals. If anyone's going to know the fishes' habits, their favourite hangouts, it's them.

However, as we all know, anglers are devious, mendacious, glinty-eyed fabricators of the facts. So: can you trust the locals? Here are some exchanges I have overhead between visiting anglers and locals.

> VISITOR: *So where's the best place to find fish around here?*
> LOCAL: **Fish? Round here?**
> VISITOR: *Yes, that's right.*
> LOCAL: **Won't find any fish round here!**
> VISITOR: *Really? But isn't this a fishing lake?*
> LOCAL: **Not so as I know of.**
> VISITOR: *But there's a sign on that gate: 'FISHING LAKE'.*
> LOCAL: **Is there?**
> VISITOR: *Yes.*
> LOCAL: [STANDS IN FRONT OF SIGN] **You must be mistaken. This sign says 'FIKE'. On account of there being a fike here.**
> VISITOR: *Look, just there – a fish rose!*
> LOCAL: **I didn't see it.**

At a trout lake, a local has just hooked his fourth fish…

> VISITOR: *What fly are you using?*
> LOCAL: **Who wants to know?**
> VISITOR: *Er. Me?*
> LOCAL: **No flies here.**
> VISITOR: *But you just caught a trout on one.*
> LOCAL: **No trout here.**
> VISITOR: *You're reeling it in as we speak!*
> LOCAL: **Don't need your sort round here.**
> VISITOR: *I hear the big fish are all up among the reeds on the far bank.*
> LOCAL: **Oooh no no no.**

VISITOR: *Really? That's what I heard.*

LOCAL: Then you heard wrong.

VISITOR: *Did I?*

LOCAL: Aye.

VISITOR: *But that's what the bailiff told me.*

LOCAL: Wouldn't trust him as far as I could throw him!

VISITOR: *I read it on the website too.*

LOCAL: Don't believe those new-fangled things.

VISITOR: *So where would you fish?*

LOCAL: I'd get in my car and I'd keep on driving, a long, long way away, then I'd fish there. Among all the other people who aren't from round these parts.

VISITOR: *Charming!*

LOCAL: You watch your tongue or I'll set one of my pot-bellied pigs on you.

VISITOR: *Run those directions past me again…*

40 THINGS YOU NEVER KNEW ABOUT OUR UNDERWATER FRIENDS

Only one of these is actually true. Can you spot which one? (Answer at the end.)

1. Chubb locks were named after chub, who guard their possessions jealously.

2. In the Wild West, a circus octopus named Sid was trained by the ringmaster to shoot eight six-guns at the same time.

3. Sid was challenged to a duel by 'Crazy' Steve McQuilty; outgunned and outclassed, McQuilty paid with his life.

4. The perch will never do a poo in front of other fish.

5. Fish names. There's a horsefish, a goatfish, a turkeyfish and a rabbitfish, but there is no warty angler.

6. Never surprise a red gurnard – when shocked, the spikes in their dorsal fin shoot out, after which, disabled, they swim round and round in circles.

7. Emperor Hojimoto of Japan, who ruled during the 7th century, was so taken with koi carp that he used to wear one as a hat.

8. The kissing gourami, a tropical fish often kept in homes, which touches lips with others of its species, is susceptible to herpes.

9. A great white caught off the coast of Australia was found to have a crocodile in its stomach. Amazingly, inside the croc's stomach was a duck-billed platypus. The platypus' last meal turned out to be a McDonald's Big Mac.

10. In real life, Sea Monkeys look exactly like they do on the box, with crowns and grins and everything.

11. Kippers got their name by falling asleep during the smoking process.

12. You can train a crab to do the hokey-cokey.

13. The monkfish never changes its expression, unless you suddenly shout, 'Hoi, Charlie!' at it, when its face comes alive with shock.

14. Which is why monkfish are believed to be reincarnated from a monk named Charlie, who possibly died because his mouth was way too big for his head.

15. Seahorses are all actual horses whose legs fell off and then they rolled into the sea.

16. Fish fingers are made from the fingerfish, which is exactly the same shape as a fish finger!

17. Peter's elephantnose fish is so-called because it has a nose like an elephant's and was first discovered by a bloke called Peter... Actually, that might be true, so try this instead: trout have guns.

18. Newcastle United striker Shola Ameobi is named after a shoal of fish and an amoeba.

19. The residents of 2541 Sienna Boulevard, Nebraska, were convinced it was raining fish, until they realized a rubbish fish juggler had moved in next door.

20. Garfish can be found in French railway stations.

21. The world's smelliest fish is the Bombay duck because it keeps warm by wearing a waistcoat made of anchovies.

22. Cod are colour-blind and cannot distinguish between red and green, which is why you should never leave one in charge of a motor vehicle.

23. No one has ever caught a mustard eel because its diet consists solely of mustard, which will fall off a hook once wet.

24. If you touch the black spot on a John Dory you will die of the plague.

25. The sarcastic fringehead is an eel-like fish that lives off the coast of California. It has never knowingly been sarcastic.

26. Steven Spielberg initially used a real shark in *Jaws*, however he changed his mind and switched to an animatronic version when it ate his first choice of lead actor, Rick Moranis.

27. Terrapins are jealous of turtles.

28. While flirting, stingray wear eggcups over their tails so they don't injure each other.

29. The world record for stuffing whitebait up one nostril is 77.

30. Leonardo da Vinci got his idea for parachutes by watching jellyfish in his local aquarium.

31. Crabs can form themselves into crab-sticks if they feel like being helpful.

32. Plankton once held a demonstration in vast numbers, waving 'PLANKTON HAVE RIGHTS TOO, YOU KNOW' placards, but the whales didn't take any notice.

33. Buster Keaton kept lobsters as pets.

34. Prawns hate each other.

35. Never eat haddock with kidney beans. If combined the two set off a chemical reaction that will result in Armageddon.

36. The singer Seal actually is a seal.

37. Take great care when gutting a conger eel – their kidneys have been known to attack humans.

38. Disney originally intended making *Finding Nemo* as live-action. It wasn't a problem finding sea creatures that could talk, it was just that none of them could act.

39. Turbot are scared of gravy boats.

40. Trapped underwater in 2005, diver Dave Stephens of Florida was kept alive by a female narwhal, who shared her air supply with him. They fell in love and later married. Dave's parents refused to attend the ceremony.

ANSWER *The only truthful statement is... number 25.*

OUTRO

So this is the end, my only friend, the end. (Channelling the ghost of Jim Morrison there.) So many lessons, so many absolutely true tales, so much wisdom imparted in such a relatively small tome. Consider yourself one of the lucky ones – other anglers might have bought a book by one of those telly anglers, who are fun to watch but don't know their stuff like I do. And don't they bang on about how great they are? Makes you sick.

I leave you with this little acronym, to keep with you every time you go fishing:

In time, with practice, you might become half the angler I am.
Many's the time you will catch nothing.

At other times, you will not (catch nothing).

Consider that yours is the sport of kings.
Or is that boxing?
Mark well these required traits of the greatest anglers:
Patience;
Learning;
Elegance;
Tenacity;
Experience;

Genius and
Idiosyncrasy.
That's all, folks!

Right, I think there's just time for the story of when I went fishing with David Bowie and his wife Iman. It was one cold Decemb... [No there isn't. Bugger off – Ed.]